D0969083

BEAUMONT AND FLETCHER

Beaumont and Fletcher

A CRITICAL STUDY

WILLIAM W. APPLETON

LONDON

GEORGE ALLEN & UNWIN LTD

RUSKIN HOUSE MUSEUM STREET

FIRST PUBLISHED IN 1956

PRINTED IN GREAT BRITAIN
in 12 point Bembo type
BY SIMSON SHAND LTD
LONDON, HERTFORD AND HARLOW

PREFACE

THE 1616 Folio of Ben Jonson, the 1623 Folio of Shakespeare, and the 1679 Folio of Beaumont and Fletcher comprise the three great treasure-houses of Elizabethan and Stuart drama. Of the three, Beaumont and Fletcher find today the fewest readers, and certainly the fewest spectators. Yet for a century readers ranked them with Jonson and Shakespeare and for a century audiences applauded their work.

It has become commonplace to dismiss them as dramatists not for all time but for an age. Yet to be successful dramatists in the age of James I, the greatest age of English drama, is scarcely an indictment, and to enjoy enormous popularity through the Restoration, the second greatest period of English drama, not a trifling commendation. We might do well, perhaps, to reconsider our current neglect of them.

It is not difficult to account, in part at least, for this neglect. The sheer quantity of their work acts as a deterrent. The fifty-two plays of the 1679 Folio make up a formidable volume. Admittedly one must sometimes pick one's way through the rubbish before coming upon the treasure, but the treasure is there, and in an age when literary reputation so often seems in inverse proportion to literary output, it can be a pleasure to lose oneself in the rich amplitude of this volume.

The predominantly bibliographical nature of many studies of Beaumont and Fletcher has perhaps also served as a deterrent. While of invaluable assistance to the scholar, they have done little to stimulate the general reader's interest. In this study I have made no attempt to deal with bibliographical problems, nor can I hide my feelings of gratitude and relief that others have done so before me. My debt to them is clear, as it is to a number of recent scholars who have approached the work of Beaumont and Fletcher from a fresh critical point of view. My purpose has been both to synthesize a good deal of this material and to suggest, at least, an approach to their plays.

I could wish that the scope of this study might allow further examination of topical allusions in their plays and a more detailed consideration of the nature of their audience. I realize also that the poverty of information on the staging in the private theatres obscures the true appreciation of Beaumont and Fletcher's achievement. All of these matters have given me pause. But the need for an over-all view of this achievement justifies, I hope, the risk of attempting such a survey.

The edition of Beaumont and Fletcher I have used for reference is that of Arnold Glover and A. R. Waller (Cambridge, 1905–12).

CONTENTS

ONE

APPRENTICE DRAMATISTS

IN 1607 Francis Beaumont and John Fletcher each presented to Ben Jonson commendatory verses to *Volpone*. The date marks the beginning of an association which culminated in the most successful collaboration in the English drama. Ben Jonson, in accepting their gratifying compliments, could hardly have guessed what formidable theatrical rivals they would subsequently prove.

On the surface there was little to differentiate them from the swarm of young Londoners of gentle birth with a pretty talent for versifying. Both were younger sons, John Fletcher, born in 1579, the fourth child of a vicar, who later became Bishop of London, and Francis Beaumont, born in 1584 or 1585, third son of one of the Queen's justices in the Court of Common Pleas. Francis Beaumont had entered Broadgates Hall, Oxford, in 1597, but left without taking a degree and subsequently studied law in the Inner Temple. He had felt no more enthusiasm for that institution than other dramatists before and after. The fashionably erotic poem, *Salmacis and Hermaphroditus*, had not rescued him from obscurity. His family's implication in the Gunpowder Plot had not improved his chances, and the failure of his first play, *The Woman Hater*, did not augur a brilliant career. For John Fletcher, in 1607, the prospect seemed even bleaker. With characteristic vacillation Elizabeth had frowned and smiled on his father, the Bishop of London, but an injudicious second marriage brought about his suspension. The melancholy bishop, so Fuller tells us, 'seeking to lose his sorrow in a mist of smoak, died of the immoderate taking thereof'. His family inherited little but his debts, and from 1596 to 1606 we know little of John Fletcher's career. Possibly he attended Corpus Christi, Cambridge. Possibly his education was entrusted to his uncle Giles Fletcher, the diplomat. He remains in the shadows until his collaboration with Beaumont begins.

When the two young bachelors took lodgings together in Southwark, some thirty years had passed since the Burbages had built, with their own hands, The Theatre in Shoreditch. Approximately ten years had passed since Shakespeare had established himself as the leading playwright for Burbage's company, The Chamberlain's Men. During that time the English theatre and English society had undergone profound, if not immediately discernible, transformations. The death of Elizabeth and the enthronement of James epitomized these changes. Gloriana had symbolized England, and in the Ditchley portrait of Elizabeth we see her literally bestriding Albion. James's relation to his Kingdom and subjects was much less assured. From Scotland he had imported a coterie of advisers and favourites who, in large measure, insulated him from Elizabeth's courtiers. The social and political cleavage between the old regime and the new was mirrored in the theatre, as Alfred Harbage has so strikingly demonstrated. The boy companies, who during the declining days of Elizabeth had enjoyed fashionable patronage, reaped a still greater success with the advent of James. Society drifted away from the open-air, public theatres on the Bankside to the enclosed private theatres used by the Children of Paul's and the Children of the Chapel and the Queen's Revels.

Not surprisingly, Beaumont and Fletcher began their dramatic apprenticeship in these private theatres. As young men of good family, they were understandably attracted by the fashionable audiences and repertories of the children's companies. At the Children of Paul's, a contemporary playgoer observed, 'A man shall not be chokte with the stench of Garlick, nor be pasted to the barmie jacket of a Beer-brewer'. There the children disported themselves ('lasciviously writhing their tender limbs,' so the Puritans charged) in the humour comedies of Chapman and Jonson and the satiric comedies of John Marston. Shakespeare and the King's Men offered *Othello* and *Lear* at the more democratic Globe in Southwark, but the popular theatres, by and large, occupied themselves with such trumpery as *If You Know Not Me You Know Nobody* or the exploits of Dick Whittington and his cat. The two young men who aspired to careers as dramatists sensibly realized that the path to success lay through the fashionable private theatres. They aspired to please an audience that preferred Marston's *Dutch Courtesan* to Dekker's *Honest Whore*, and in the comedies of humour and the satires Beaumont found his model for his first play, the comedy of *The Woman Hater*.

Generally felt to be entirely by Beaumont, with some possible assistance from Fletcher, *The Woman Hater* was produced by the Children of Paul's some time before their dissolution in 1606. The mocking prologue, disclaiming any satirical or bawdy intent, perfectly sets the tone of the play. The plot is, as usual in Beaumont and Fletcher, a double one. Lazarillo, a gourmet-courtier, stricken with a humour for the head of an Umbranoe-fish, pursues this delicacy from court to mercer's shop to stews where his anxiety to sample this rarity leads him into marriage with a whore. The main plot centres on Gondarino, an old soldier and woman-hater, who, angered by the light-hearted Oriana, manœuvres her into a bawdy house. There, before the Duke and the Count, her brother, he attempts to prove her licentiousness. His demonstration fails, however, and the Duke, commending her virtue, offers her his own hand. The action, though purportedly occurring in Milan, clearly takes place in the London of the troubled early years of James's reign.

On the surface this moderately applauded comedy seems little more than a Chapman-Jonson comedy of humours with perhaps some tincture of Middleton's city comedies—*A Trick to Catch the Old One* and *Michaelmas Term*—also written for the Paul's Boys. But the quality of Beaumont's humours and the tone of his play show marked individuality and clearly suggest later works in the Beaumont and Fletcher canon.

Gondarino, in the first place, marks a departure from the conventional humour types. By contrasting him with the central figure in Jonson's later comedy, *Epicoene* (1609), we can perhaps grasp something of the peculiar cast of Beaumont's conception. In Jonson's play Morose, a confirmed bachelor, passionately antipathetic to noise and turmoil, finds that he has been tricked into marriage with a brawling Xantippe. He wins his release from her only by restoring to favour his disinherited nephew, who then exposes Morose's wife as a boy in disguise. A trick has been played. The comic price of gullibility has been exacted. The comedy of the conclusion of *The Woman Hater* differs markedly from this. As a climactic punishment for his slander, Gondarino is tied in a chair, and Oriana taunts him until he turns savagely upon her.

Gond.: Mayst thou be quickly old and painted; mayst thou dote upon some sturdy yeoman of the woodyard and may he be honest; mayst thou be barred the lawful lechery of thy coach for want of instruments; and last, be thy womb unopened.
Duke: This fellow hath a pretty gaul.
Count: My Lord, I hope to see him purged e'r he part.
(V, 2)

It is a consummation as devoutly to be wished as it is unlikely to be fulfilled. His cry in the concluding scene as a teasing circle of ladies surround him and offer to kiss him: 'No, sear my lips with hot irons first,' carries him beyond the comfortable borders of comedy. Gondarino's final words (the text is clearly in error and the next to the last speech belongs not to Gondarino but the Count) show his purgation uneffected. While Oriana blithely probes the extent of Gondarino's *horror feminae* the Duke complacently observes: 'She tortures him admirably'. Granted that an extrovert audience might have reacted to this as robust comedy—as less sophisticated audiences have received, for example, the film versions of Tennessee Williams' plays—Beaumont's last scene nonetheless gives one pause. On the whole it is somewhat strong fare for modern readers who would probably prove equally squeamish before that other form of Tudor and Stuart amusement, bear-baiting, which the last scene of Beaumont's comedy so strongly suggests.

The misogynistic abuse of women—'that were created only for the preservation of little dogs'—later to become a commonplace in Fletcher's work—also goes far to prove that the Comic Muse wears many faces. Doubtless these attacks, an inheritance from Juvenal and the Elizabethan satires on women's painting and lechery, had in their time a topical appeal for the epicene court of James. But Gondarino, as a comic conception, has, for us, a disturbing ambivalence. The portrait of him—half-perverse, half-comic, justifies Beaumont's admission in the Prologue: 'I dare not call it a comedy or tragedy'. Artistically he fails. Gondarino is both the Thurber hero and the Strindberg martyr in the battle of the sexes.

Oriana also has this same ambivalence. In her bedevilment of Gondarino she suggests the comic *Venus predatorix* of Restoration comedy. She partakes also of her moral ambiguity. Manipulating her into an equivocal position in a bordello, Gondarino—and Beaumont—exploit her situation as fully as possible. She remains *virgo intacta,* but she has little of the purity of those two other sin-encompassed heroines, Peele's Delia in the *Old Wives' Tale* or her younger sister, Milton's Lady in *Comus*. Her behaviour justifies, in large measure, Coleridge's observation that Beaumont and Fletcher's heroines are either strumpets or virgins with the minds of strumpets. Though liveliness and wit do much to redeem her, they are insufficient to lift her to a high comic plane. Oriana's artifices call to mind the machinations of Clarissa Harlowe rather than the witty stratagems of Millamant or Ann Whitefield.

As a prose comedy of contemporary London the play has undeniable interest.[1] Beaumont's satire leaves none unscathed from the foolish mercer to the ambitious courtier. For the citizenry he has good-natured contempt; for the court circle he feels scarcely more reverence. In the farcical embroglio over the Umbranoe's head and the subsequent arrest of Lazarillo for treason, he satirizes the intrigues of the Gunpowder Plot and the subsequent rumours and investigations which involved Beaumont's own family. Both in content and form this play indicates Beaumont's desire to make use of the current scene and current literary fashions. His attempt to approximate the Chapman-Jonson humours and the mocking laughter of Marston's comedies (The Dutch Courtesan, Franceschina, finds her namesake in *The Woman Hater*) show how eager he was to attune himself to theatrical fashion.

The Knight of the Burning Pestle (1607–10?) is marked by this same eclecticism, this same pervasive satire. We recognize it now as a masterpiece among dramatic burlesques, but Beaumont, while he found in this *genre* a brilliant medium for his talents, misjudged his audience. *The Knight of the Burning Pestle* anticipated a later audience and a later theatre. Though Beaumont and Fletcher subsequently became famous, or infamous, through their sense of fashion, *The Knight of the Burning Pestle* is a miscalculation. Earlier, during the satiric War of the Theatres (1599–1601), it might have enjoyed some success. But if it came some five years too late, it came also at least five years too early.

Its failure when presented by the Children of the Queen's Revels, before the select Blackfriars audience, has been accounted for in diametrically opposed fashion.[2] Hazelton Spencer has suggested that the critical satire was resented by the citizenry. Alfred Harbage denies this by pointing out that the citizens were not in the audience, and that the exceptional moderation of the satire probably accounted for its failure. The latter is the more plausible reason. The audiences of Blackfriars and the Globe, though socially differentiated, had much in common. The cleavage between the popular and private theatres had not yet deepened enough so that this satire of the citizens' easy-going critical attitudes could be understood and properly relished, as it was by the more sophisticated spectators in later Jacobean and Caroline audiences.

But it is this moderation, this fundamental humaneness and good sense which lift *The Knight of the Burning Pestle* above all other dramatic burlesques, with the exception of *The Critic*. In making fun of the school of Dekker and Heywood and the Palmerin romance, Beaumont writes without the astringency and bitterness of Marston or Jonson, and the generality of his satire of taste absolves his play from the pettiness and topicality that mar Villiers' *The Rehearsal*.

The opening scene, as lively and life-like as Christopher Sly's induction to *The Taming of the Shrew*, introduces us to a grocer, his wife, and their apprentice, Ralph, taking their places in an audience gathered to witness a play about a London merchant. Deferring to the spectators' wishes, the players agree to make Ralph the hero of the play, and the wills of his doting guardians dictate his subsequent adventures. In part suggested by Peele's *The Old Wives' Tale*, and in part perhaps by Cervantes' incomparable *Don Quixote*,[3] the play describes how Ralph helps Jasper win the hand of Luce. Wandering from the solid bourgeois haunts of London to Waltham Forest and the King of Moldavia's palace, which the grocer's wife wishes to see appropriately 'covered with black velvet', Ralph satirizes Heywood's apprentice heroes, as Merrythought and his shrewish wife satirize Dekker's citizenry. That Beaumont scarcely exaggerated the tastes of the popular audience and its occasional obstreperousness may be judged from a somewhat later document cited by Leslie Hotson:

> I have known upon one of these *Festivals*, but especially at *Shrove-tide*, where the Players have been appointed, notwithstanding their bils to the contrary, to act what the major part of the company had a mind to; sometimes *Tamerlane*, sometimes *Jugurth*, sometimes the Jew of *Malta*, and sometimes parts of all of these, and at last, none of the three taking, they were forced to undresse and put off their Tragick habits, and conclude the day with the merry milkmaides. And unlesse this were done, . . . as sometimes it so fortun'd, that the Players were refractory; the Benches, the tiles, the laths, the stones, Oranges, Apples, Nuts, flew about most liberally, and as there were Mechanicks of all professions, who fell everyone to his owne trade, and dissolved a house in an instant, and make a ruine of a stately Fabrick.[4]

The grocer and his wife, though less boisterous, are critically cousin to this audience. But their good humour, and Beaumont's, save the play. He shows a sympathy for the variety and richness of the fare in the popular theatres. His sunny tolerance and detached amusement call to mind the great French comic master who could at once cherish and satirize the bourgeoisie. Monsieur Jourdain is a more prosperous version of the grocer, and Beaumont and Molière share much the same attitude toward their subjects. Even Heywood and Dekker's glorifications of the London apprentices partake of this same laughter. Their young heroes smell of the streets and shops of London. They have the solidity of Sancho Panza, yet they move in the world of Don Quixote. They epitomize both the hardheadedness and high imagination of the Elizabethan age. Beaumont's skill in satirically mixing these elements can be illustrated in the final scene when Ralph, commanded to 'come away quickly and die,' makes his absurd farewell. Only a few years earlier the strutting heroes of the chronicles had gone out of favour; with Ralph's demise the legend of glorious apprentices falls into decay. The almost hermaphroditic hero of Beaumont and Fletcher stands backstage, waiting to take his place.

Beaumont's play is a comic valedictory. He has his laugh at the *naïveté* and rough manners of the citizenry in the public theatres, but his satire is as reluctant as it is tempered, and there is an irresistible poignancy in the farewell of the grocer and his wife to the audience.

> *Cit.:* Come *Nell*, shall we go, the Play's done?
>
> *Wife:* Nay, by my faith *George*, I have more manners than so, I'll speak to these Gentlemen first: I thank you all Gentlemen, for your patience and countenance to *Ralph*, a poor fatherless child, and if I may see you at my house, it should go hard, but I would have a pottle of Wine, and a Pipe of Tobacco for you; for truly I hope you [do] like the youth, but I would be glad to know the truth: I refer it to your own discretions, whether you will applaud him or no, for I will wink, and whilst you shall do what you will, I thank you with all my heart, God give you good night, come *George*.
>
> (V, 1)

If Beaumont had his early disappointments, Fletcher had his also. Performance by the Children of the Queen's Revels and praise from Jonson and Chapman could not atone for the hisses with which the audience received his first play, *The Faithful Shepherdess* (1608–09). Like Beaumont, in *The Knight of the Burning Pestle*, he misjudged his audience. Only after the *longueurs* of D'Urfé's *L'Astrée* (1610–27) had become fashionable, and only after the establishment of Queen Henrietta Maria's cult of love, did the play enjoy favour. Even then its success was limited, and Davenant's revised version of 1633 received no more than polite and scattered applause.

Why it failed can be at least in part explained. Fletcher himself accounted for it as resulting from the audience's expectation of 'a play of country hired shepherds in gray cloaks, with curtailed dogs in strings, sometimes laughing together and sometimes killing one another'. It is hard to conceive what entertainments either he, or the audience, had in mind. His definition does not fit the stately pastorals of Daniel, and though it vaguely calls to mind Jonson's *The Sad Shepherd,* the latter was discovered in fragmentary form only after Jonson's death.

On the surface, Fletcher's play relates to Guarini's *Il Pastor Fido* (1585), but the resemblance scarcely goes beyond that. 'Neither plot, situation or characters imitate foreign models,'[5] writes Ristine, concurring with Fleay who felt that Fletcher rivalled rather than imitated Tasso and Guarini. But for the definition of tragi-comedy contained in the Preface to *The Faithful Shepherdess* Fletcher is clearly indebted to Guarini.

> A tragi-comedie is not so called in respect of mirth and killing, but in respect it wants deaths, which is inough to make it no tragedie, yet brings some neere it, which is inough to make it no comedie: which must be a representation of familiar people, with such kinde of trouble as no life be questiond, so that a God is as lawfull in this as in a Tragedie, and meane people as in a comedie.

This emphasis on tragi-comedy as a mean between tragedy and comedy, on its lack of deaths, and on the varied station of its characters suggests that Fletcher was well acquainted with the controversy between Guarini and Giasone de Nores in which the former championed the legitimacy of the new *genre*. Fletcher echoes the definition of tragi-comedy contained in the belligerent *Il Verato Secondo*. . . .[6] It serves as the basis for many of the later tragi-comedies, but has distinctly less application to *The Faithful Shepherdess*. Small wonder that this play puzzled Fletcher's audience. It is neither a comedy, nor a tragedy, nor a pastoral—as they knew it. It would have defied even that master of dramatic definition, Polonius. It relates most closely, perhaps, not to Guarini, or Daniel, or English folk-play, but to Spenser.

Throughout the play names echo from *The Shepheards Calender*, and strong reminiscences of the Third Book of *The Faerie Queene*, the Book of Chastity, underlie Fletcher's work.

The play, complex as its intrigue is, can be reduced to a single theme. The theme is love, and the variations of love, and the *dramatis personae* make up a spectrum of lovers. The scene lies in the night-time woods of Thessaly, and during the first act Fletcher introduces us to these lovers, sacred and profane. Chief among the former is Clorin, as pure as the exquisite lady of Milton's *Comus*, and so dedicated to the memory of her dead love that she has effected in herself a complete purgation from 'all heats and fires of love'. Around this immovable central figure the action of the play revolves, and through her the purgation and final resolution take place. Her companions of the fields and woods vary from the chaste Perigot and Amoret to the more sensual Amaryllis, the frankly lustful Cloe and Sullen Shepherd, and, coming full circle, the virtuous Alexis, fired by hopeless love for Clorin. All of these, from the purest lover to the most corrupt voluptuary, Fletcher carefully juxtaposes, and through Amarillis' transformations into the seeming Amoret he develops a series of violently contrasted scenes, with Perigot alternately attracted by the chaste virtues of the real Amoret and repelled by the lustful advances of the false one.[7]

Superficially the play has much in common with *A Midsummer Night's Dream*. Both plays are nocturnes, with their scene in Thessaly, and in both distracted lovers lose themselves in the forest where their relationships shift and change under the power of magic. Clorin's faithful satyr has some resemblance to Puck. But Shakespeare's play is a romance on many levels ranging from the sophisticated nuptials of Theseus and Hippolyta to the mirthful tragedy of Pyramus and Thisbe and the amorous complications of the quartet of young Athenians. His play is drenched in the music, moonlight and dews of the summer night, but it echoes also with the robust laughter of the Athenian tradesmen. In Fletcher's world, keyed in silver, Bottom has no place. He plants his feet too firmly on the ground; he belongs outside Fletcher's hierarchy of lovers who, Platonist to satyr, all share a common abstractness. Fletcher's use of the unities of time and place further demonstrates the formality of his conception. The play lends itself easily to the classical Serlio satyric setting, with its rude bower and woods, and the time covers the period from late afternoon until sunrise, an exact inversion of Guarini's time-plot.

In a number of ways the play suggests the later work of Beaumont and Fletcher. The ever-present threat of tragedy and the love-lust opposition that dominate tragi-comedy are both strongly evident. Repeatedly *The Faithful Shepherdess* foreshadows *Philaster*. Perigot's obsession with the loftiest concepts of love relates him to the absolutists of tragi-comedy. The slightest deviation in Amoret's behaviour from the conduct imposed by these ideals drives him almost to madness. Tortured by the vision of the false Amoret, he strikes and wounds his beloved, as Philaster does. Perigot shares with the protagonists of tragi-comedy a shrill, hysterical quality. Cloe foreshadows the lustful ladies to come, and Clorin the Platonic heroines.

The Faithful Shepherdess betrays Fletcher's youth. The characters in his study of the ways of love have neither the absolute formality, the two-dimensionality of playing-cards, nor the third-dimensionality of flesh and blood. They stand somewhere in between, like the uncomfortable figures in allegorical Renaissance tapestries. His language, though marked by exquisitely modulated lyricism, is essentially non-dramatic. *The Faithful Shepherdess* suffers also from its over-formalized pattern. Perigot's alternating joy and despair can be charted like an undulant fever. The machinations of Cloe soon become wearisome. By the close of the first act the changes have all been rung. The ensuing acts are merely echoes. Fletcher had not as yet mastered the highly wrought situation, the change of pace in language, and the variety of scene that stamp the later plays.

Cupid's Revenge is in many ways a reaction against the earlier play. Published in 1615, it was performed by the Children of the Queen's Revels at Blackfriars sometime between 1607–12. How much of a hand Beaumont had in its authorship is conjectural. Few doubt that the major part of the play, if not all of it, belongs to Fletcher, for it shows his continuing preoccupation with the theme and schematized pattern of *The Faithful Shepherdess*.

The plot and subplot he found in that El Dorado of Elizabethan source material, Sidney's *Arcadia*. From the second book Fletcher drew two stories: Erona's dethronement of Cupid and her subsequent love for Antiphilus, and the account of Prince Plangus' love for a private man's wife. The latter story, a variant on the legend of Joseph and Potiphar's wife, Fletcher appropriated with few alterations. The other story, however, Fletcher conspicuously changed, and it provides an interesting example of his early dramatic methods. Both Sidney and Fletcher begin with the same premise. Angered by the Princess Erona's commands to overthrow his altars, Cupid punishes her by causing her to fall violently in love. At this point their stories diverge. In Fletcher's play the Princess Hidaspes (Erona) falls in love not with a young man 'of mean parentage . . . the sonne of her Nurse' (Antiphilus) but with Zoilus, the court dwarf. 'This comes of chastity,' one of the courtiers placidly observes. Driven frantic when her angry father kills the dwarf, she herself dies. Her *recherché* sexual cravings and the grotesque curiosity of her situation have a certain shock value, but they do not lend themselves to much dramatic development. The Princess Hidaspes makes her entrance in the first act, Cupid's curse takes its effect, and after the second act she disappears.

The story, as Sidney tells it, though far less sensational, has far more dramatic possibilities.[8] Antiphilus, beloved by the Princess Erona, is overcome in combat by Prince Plangus and imprisoned. At the cost of an unwanted marriage to Tiridates, Erona is offered her lover's release. The wish to save her lover and her reluctance to surrender herself to another man confront her with a cruel decision. Later on in his career Fletcher would unquestionably have seized upon this situation and highlighted this dilemma. The problem which allows no resolution, the deadlock—these are among his most effective materials, and his skill in maintaining and even heightening suspense in situations of this kind he demonstrates masterfully in such later plays as *The Maid's Tragedy* and *A King and No King*.

Two scenes alone in *Cupid's Revenge* indicate his strong dramatic instinct: Bacha's attempted seduction of her stepson Leucippus (III) and Urania's pathetic attempts to comfort the harried Leucippus (V). They represent the two emotional extremes at which Fletcher is happiest—lustful, predatory love, and wistful, dedicated love. Actually they are two sides of the same coin. Both Bacha and Urania suffer from unsatisfied love, a malady most incident to Fletcher's women.

In spite of five deaths, the play lacks tragic impact. The machinations both of Cupid and Fletcher reduce the characters to mere puppets. The Princess Hidaspes who, like Clorin, has tried to dedicate herself to Platonic love, suffers the curse of Cupid and wastes away; the chaste Urania, daughter of the unchaste Bacha, dies for love; Leucippus and Leontius also swell the catalogue of love's martyrs. As *The Faithful Shepherdess* tells the story of love's purification, *Cupid's Revenge* describes its degradation. The fascination exercised by the dwarf Zoilus upon Hidaspes symbolizes the terrible power of this love. She is as blinded to his deformity as Leucippus and Leontius are to the moral deformity behind Bacha's mask of virtue.

In action and psychology the play moves convulsively, without scenes of transition. The psychological *scène à faire* (actually rare in Elizabethan drama outside of Shakespeare) is almost always lacking in Beaumont and Fletcher. They concern themselves with the heights and depths of human experience. The valleys and plains, the sloping uplands, have little interest for them. On the stage, such omission can be condoned. Emotional ellipsis of this sort may even conceivably recommend itself. On the page, however, this broken continuity is far more disturbing. But neither on the stage, nor on the page, can *Cupid's Revenge* be accounted satisfying.

From one set of extremes Fletcher had gone to another. In place of the almost glassy, meditative verse of *The Faithful Shepherdess* he substitutes the loosest of blank verse that remains so largely by courtesy of the typesetter and more often than not breaks down into colloquial prose. He removes his scene from the artificial world of Thessaly to the corrupt court of Lycia which, with its love-sick king and scheming sycophants, calls to mind the court of James I. For his inspiration in depicting this he turned not to a fashionable continental poet, but to a native dramatist.

The corrupt court of Lycia suggests, at least, the court of Elsinore, and occasional unmistakable echoes of Shakespeare ring out: 'Live, wicked mother; that reverend Title be your pardon, for I will use no extremity against you, but leave you to Heaven'. (V, 1.) But the analogy between the two plays cannot be pressed. Leucippus, Leontius and Bacha have only the most shadowy resemblance to Hamlet, Claudius and Gertrude. The parallels are worth citing, slight as they may be, only because they indicate Beaumont and Fletcher's early interest in Shakespeare and *Hamlet*, in particular. With *Philaster* these parallels have more consequence.

Behind *Cupid's Revenge* and the other early plays of Beaumont and Fletcher one senses an uneasiness and restless experimentation. But the decade from 1600–1610 is one of transition and change in the theatre, its audience and repertory. In bringing about these changes Ben Jonson, perhaps more than any other individual, played a major part. Despite all his services to the English drama, he can be cited for conspicuous disservice as well. He did much to divide the audience. His sense of the function of the theatre did not accord with the opinions of the clapper-clawing mob, and he was proud of it. His concepts of tragedy and comedy were, fundamentally, as aristocratic as those of Sidney, and his impulse the same—to prevent the spontaneous and undisciplined growth of the drama. Instead, so he felt, the drama needed the fertilization of the classics and the pruning shears of Aristotle.

Chapman's *A Humorous Day's Mirth* (1597) inaugurated a type of comedy that Jonson codified in *Every Man in His Humour* (1598) and a subsequent series of satirical comedies for the private theatres. In *Sejanus* (1603) he attempted to do as much for tragedy. Its failure embittered him, and his preliminary letter to the 1605 edition of the play shows the author in one of his most belligerent and least attractive moods. 'It is a poeme, that . . . suffer'd not lesse violence from our people here, then the subiect of it did from the rage of the people of Rome.' Again and again Jonson's snarling prefaces indicate his contempt for the audience. His tragedies pleased few. The tone of the critical comedies at least partially alienated popular audiences. Less sophisticated than the spectators in the private theatres, and more certain in their moral judgments, they persisted in their fondness for such fare as *Mucedorus* and romantic comedy.

Other factors as well contributed to the growing schism in the audience. Periodic closings because of the plague during the years 1605–1610 sapped the vitality of the theatre. The remote locations of The Red Bull and The Fortune, built during the first years of the century, discouraged fashionable spectators who increasingly patronized the convenient theatres of Blackfriars and Whitefriars, while the prices of admission at these private theatres, in turn, discouraged the humbler section of the playgoing public. James's autocratic outlook and disposition did little to lessen the breach between London and Westminster, and the theatres which had boasted truly democratic audiences during the sixteenth century increasingly catered to less representative ones. The Restoration audience of 1660, the most narrow and specialized in the history of the English theatre, is anticipated in the aristocratic audiences of the private theatres during the reigns of the early Stuarts. When the theatres closed in 1642, London already had three predominantly private theatres.

During the early stages of this schism Beaumont and Fletcher served their dramatic apprenticeship. During this time also the concept of tragi-comedy slowly evolved.[9] Chapman's *The Gentleman Usher* (1602) rather strikingly anticipates the Guarini-Fletcher definition of this *genre:* 'It wants deaths, which is inough to make it no tragedie, yet brings some near it, which is inough to make it no comedie'. Through the agency of a supernaturally gifted physician, Chapman succeeds in steering this treacherous middle course. His heroine, her beauty eaten away by poison, is miraculously restored to radiant bloom; his hero, fatally wounded, enjoys a similarly miraculous restoration. Chapman's *The Widow's Tears* (1605) also hovers between comedy and tragedy, and Shakespeare during these years occupies himself with the perplexing 'problem' comedies, *All's Well That Ends Well* and *Measure For Measure*. Marston's *The Malcontent* (printed in 1604 but probably played in 1601) significantly appears on The Stationers' Register as a tragi-comedy. Its mixed tonality strikingly suggests the work of Beaumont and Fletcher. The potentially macabre constantly dissolves into Hallowe'en foolery and burlesque. In varying degrees all these plays contributed to the later successes of Beaumont and Fletcher.

Their own first works, however uneven, also served a purpose. Beaumont and Fletcher learned much from their failures, their inability to gauge the temper and the tastes of their audience. In tragi-comedy they found the ideal medium for their talents and the ideal entertainment for their audience. As Giraudoux remarks: 'En fait, chaque théâtre n'est bâti que pour une seule pièce, et le seul secret de sa direction est de découvrir laquelle'.[10] With *Philaster* the collaborators discovered this play.

NOTES TO CHAPTER ONE

1. Albert W. Upton, 'Allusions to James I and his Court in *The Woman Hater*,' *Modern Language Association Publications*, XLIV (1929), pp. 1048–1065.
2. Alfred Harbage, *Shakespeare and the Rival Traditions*, New York, 1952, p. 107.
3. Herbert S. Murch, ed., *The Knight of the Burning Pestle*, Yale Studies in English, XXXIII, New York, 1908, pp. xxxii–lviii.
4. Leslie Hotson, *The Commonwealth and Restoration Stage*, Cambridge, Mass., 1928, p. 45.
5. Frank H. Ristine, *English Tragicomedy*, New York, 1910, p. 108.
6. Guarini, *Opere*, Verona, 1737–1738, III, 167.
7. Eugene M. Waith, *The Pattern of Tragicomedy in Beaumont and Fletcher*, New Haven, 1952, pp. 5–11.
8. Sir Philip Sidney, *Arcadia*, Lib. 2, Chapters 12–13.
9. Ristine, *Tragicomedy*, pp. 60–111; Madeleine Doran, *Endeavours of Art*, Madison, Wisconsin, 1954, pp. 186–215.
10. *Ondine*, II, 1.

TWO

THE COLLABORATION

BY 1608 the vogue for the children's companies had virtually come to an end, and some two hundred years elapsed before the success of Master Betty inspired further little eyases. After 1606 the Paul's Boys were no longer active and in 1608, the Children of the Queen's Revels, previously rebuked for *Eastward Ho,* were silenced for some injudicious mockery of the court in Chapman's *Conspiracy and Tragedy of Charles, Duke of Byron.* They surrendered the lease of Blackfriars to Richard Burbage. The Globe subsequently became the home of the King's Men from May to November and Blackfriars their headquarters during the winter months.

The importance of this development can scarcely be too much emphasized, and Gerald Bentley has acutely pointed out its implications.[1] For the first time an adult company was to occupy one of the private theatres, hitherto the exclusive province of the children's companies. It became their office to amuse a courtly audience whose taste differed enough from that of the Globe audience to render much of the repertory useless. For these spectators the playwrights of the King's Men devised the tragicomedy, a *genre* conditioned by the peculiar nature of its audience far more than by critical theory. As far back as *The Second Shepherds Play* English audiences had relished the mixture of the sacred and the profane, the comic and the serious. Fletcher, aware as he was of Guarini's definition of tragi-comedy, attuned himself to his audience rather than to the niceties of fashionable critical discussion.

The curious nature of tragi-comedy in more ways than one reflects the fragmentation of the old Tudor society and the emergence of the new social order to which tragi-comedy catered. During Elizabeth's reign society had centred in the court. No permanent London society or season had as yet become established. The great houses—Knole, Hatfield, Penshurst, Wilton—which studded the countryside resembled minor duchies whose power Elizabeth carefully observed and held in check through her progresses, those ruinously expensive official tours. During the reign of James I the attempt was made to establish a London season, and though the Star Chamber quickly suppressed this movement, it paved the way for the emergence of a permanent London society during the time of Charles I.

As early as 1608 Wilton and Penshurst symbolized a decaying way of life, Audley End and Ham House an increasingly dominant one. While during her reign Elizabeth had severely limited the number of titles, James doubled their number. The newly-created peers had little of the Tudor sense of *noblesse oblige*, and in Sir Giles Overreach Massinger epitomized all that he detested in the Stuart *nouveaux riches* that swarmed around the court of the new monarch. Brought up under the generous patronage of the Pembrokes, Massinger reacted keenly to the displacement of the land-poor Elizabethan nobility by the new class of projectors and monopolists. The cleavage between the old landed aristocracy and the new city aristocracy foreshadowed the war to come and the Restoration antagonism between town and country. During the period of Beaumont and Fletcher the decline of the great country household was already under way. By the time of the Restoration it was complete—country estates had become mere sources of income for absentee owners, convenient dumping-places for wives, or havens of retirement during political storms or the ravages of the gout.

The fissure in the larger units of Elizabethan society, so evident in the Jacobean drama, can be demonstrated as well in the decreasing dramatic emphasis on the smaller social unit of the family. In the plays of Beaumont and Fletcher the home, the hearth and the double bed no longer comprise the norm as they do in most earlier drama. The works of the two collaborators herald their eventual displacement by their Restoration equivalents—the chocolate-house, the salon, and the chaise longue. In their tragi-comedies the family has begun to disappear. The grocer, his wife and their beloved apprentice Ralph have vanished.

Children virtually desert the drama for a hundred years, except for their presence in occasional tableaux. (In *All for Love* Dryden allows them one word of dialogue—'Father!') From the time of Jonson on, comedy increasingly ends not in marriage for love and for children, but in a match for money and power.

Evidence of the disintegration of Tudor society into the highly competitive, individualistic Stuart society can be found in Jacobean music and domestic architecture, as well as in the drama. Architectural changes in the great houses during the first decade of the century clearly suggest these transformations. The great central inner court, the nerve centre of the Tudor household, gave way to the formal outer court. The Great Hall, the inner centre of household life, also vanished, its functions assigned to various other newly created rooms. The servants disappeared into a separate wing. The baronial unity of the medieval household was displaced by a new hierarchy with clear demarcations and delimitations.

Similarly, the trend in music indicates this process of dissolution. From 1500 to 1600 England had enjoyed a period of greatness in an outpouring of music she has never since matched. The dramas of the 1590's abound with song, and Peacham's *Compleat Gentleman* gives proof of the importance attached to music as a social grace. The necessity of bearing one's part needed no stressing, for the Elizabethan madrigal and motet were primarily social amusements. Their polyphonic structure demanded group participation. Though the madrigal remained alive during the reign of James I, an increasing interest in solo singing became marked during this period. But the deaths of William Byrd in 1623, Orlando Gibbons in 1625, John Dowland in 1626 and John Bull in 1628 brought the earlier era to a close. With the coming of Charles I music developed in an altogether different direction. The rise of Italian opera and the success of Monteverdi stimulated the homophonic and monodic style that supplanted the earlier polyphonic one. Both movements, in domestic architecture and music, are at least symptomatic of the unweaving of the strands in the hitherto tightly-knit social fabric.

The divisions that characterized the age no less stigmatized the audience for which Beaumont and Fletcher wrote. The letters of

Sir John Harington, in particular, illuminate the complexity of this court and its monarch. His account of James, 'the wisest fool in Christendom', epitomizes its paradoxes and contradictions. A notorious coward who huddled in quilted robes to protect him from the assassin's dagger, James at the same time took an almost pathological pleasure in the hunt. The lions and their whelps in the Tower both terrified and fascinated him. He could spout divinity with his most pedantic bishop or outcurse the coarsest soldier in his army.

In the Rubens ceiling at Whitehall Charles I suitably immortalized the memory of his father. The triumphant baroque allegory of the central panel of the Banqueting Hall, depicting James soaring heavenward on the wings of the eagle of Justice, suitably apotheosizes him. The flamboyant posturing of Rubens' subjects, the balletic *haute école* strut of their horses, coincided with James's own fondness for self-display. He shared the Tudor passion for dress, and his fantastic and ill-judged vanity in many ways matched the Virgin Queen's. Praise of his hounds and roan jennet paved the way to favour, and woe to the courtier who omitted to compliment his gilt stirrups. Yet in spite of his vanity, his pedantry, his foibles—a smouldering detestation of tobacco and witches—he had another side to his nature. More than once he proved a shrewd politician. Under his aegis that noble monument of English prose, the 1611 Bible, appeared.

Much the same duality marked the court itself. Its brutality Harington suggests to us in his account of a performance of 'Solomon his Temple and the Coming of the Queen of Sheba'. During its presentation both actors and spectators surrendered to the spirit of Bacchanal. Charity made obeisance before the King and then 'returned to Hope and Faith who were both sick and spewing in the lower hall'. Such strange pageantries led the ordinary high-spirited Sir John to sober meditations on the whole nature of court life:

> I have passed much time in seeing the royal sports of hunting and hawking, where the manners were such as made one devise the beasts were pursuing the sober creation and not men in quest of exercise or food. I will here, in good sooth, declare to

> you, who will not blab, that the Gunpowder Fight is got out of all our heads, and we are going on, hereabouts, as if the devil was contriving every man should blow up himself, by wild riot, excess, and devestation of time and temperance. The great ladies do go well-masked, and indeed it be the only show of their modesty, to conceal their countenances, but alack they meet with such countenance to uphold their strange doings, that I marvel nought at ought that happens.[2]

Harington's account of this court with 'beast in view' perfectly hits off the temper of the times. Robert Carr had begun his dangerous climb as favourite. The Howards were already playing deeply to strengthen the power of their faction. The stage was set for the later scandals which indelibly marked James's reign.

Against such a background and for such an audience the playwrights of the King's Men devised that hybrid entertainment, tragi-comedy. Its mixed tone, its tensions, its paradoxes and surprises relate to contemporary society rather than to literary precedent. Quite understandably the King's Men called upon Beaumont and Fletcher to provide dramatic entertainment for this audience. Their social status, previous experience at Blackfriars, and growing sense of the theatrical milieu all qualified them to do so. Until then they had tasted little success, but the triumphant production of *Philaster* justified the company's decision and resulted in the lasting association of Beaumont and Fletcher and the King's Men. The exact date of its first performance remains unknown, but it occurred some time between 1608 and October, 1610. The exact nature of the collaborative effort also remains unknown, but most critics agree that Beaumont had the major share in its authorship.

Clearly *Philaster* relates both to *The Faithful Shepherdess* and *Cupid's Revenge*, but it improves upon the first by discarding the undramatic pastoral trappings, and on the second by its incomparably better dialogue and far more interesting treatment of situation. In plot it has the schematic conception of *The Faithful Shepherdess* with two neatly designed triangles, one composed of virtuous characters—Arethusa, Philaster and Bellario—and the other made up of the activating villains of the piece—the King,

Megra and Pharamond. Though the play draws upon themes expressed in their own earlier plays and indicates the collaborators' interest in Shakespeare (*Hamlet, Othello* and *Julius Caesar* all can be discerned in *Philaster*)—its story is basically an original one. Philaster, pretender to the throne of Sicily, falls in love with the princess Arethusa, but Megra, through her evil machinations, leads him to believe that Arethusa has betrayed him with her page Bellario. Like Perigot, Philaster vacillates between elation and despair. As in the earlier play, the discrepancy between things as they are and things as they appear leads to endless complications only resolved in a final *coup de théâtre* when Bellario reveals herself as a girl and a successful revolt restores Philaster to the throne that rightfully belongs to him. Though the play comes at times close to tragedy, it ends with the triumph of love, Megra's banishment, and the tyrant dispossessed. Only Bellario's wistful presence casts a shadow on the scene of general rejoicing.

The Sicily of Theocritus which Arethusa's name evokes has undergone a transformation. We have moved away from the lanscapes of the Greek pastoralist, and left behind also Sidney's Arcadia and Shakespeare's Arden. The steadfast figures of Sidney's Basilius and Shakespeare's benevolent Duke, holding his court in the sunny fastnesses of the forest, have no place in the world of Beaumont and Fletcher.

We have returned to the Error's Wood of *The Faerie Queene* and *The Faithful Shepherdess,* but the symbolism in the tragicomedy runs deeper and has more tragic implications. Clorin and her bower have vanished. Philaster has strayed into the no-man's-land of the dispossessed. As John Danby has pointed out in his brilliantly suggestive essay, he epitomizes the dilemma of the Cavalier age. Philaster is the lost prince in search of an absolute.[3]

His problem can be strikingly demonstrated by comparing him to Shakespeare's Hamlet, with whom he has, at the beginning of the play at least, much in common. Both have lost a father, a throne rightfully theirs, and both suffer the pangs and complications of love. There the resemblance ends. Hamlet finds himself in a too-too solid (or sullied) world, but it is a world which has its values, however distorted they may be. Philaster's world of clashing absolutes lacks even this pernicious order, and he himself lacks the vision to comprehend his plight. Without Hamlet's intense perception, he seems little more than an astigmatic version of the Prince of Denmark. He senses rather than reasons. As a claimant to the throne, faced with the problem of ousting the usurper, he can neither accept nor reject the doctrine of divine right. Similarly, the Petrarchan concept of love alternately exhilarates and depresses him. Numbed by a sort of *aboulia,* he swings from one extreme to another, as circumstances dictate, in a series of scenes of violent emotional foreshortening. With Philaster it is all or nothing.

Arethusa, like him, seems powerless in a disordered world. In her first scene with Philaster she remarks:

> But spend not hasty time,
> In seeking how I came thus: 'tis the gods,
> The gods, that make me so.
>
> (I, 1)

Passion, not reason, governs her life also. Her surrender of will calls to mind the agonized cry of Phèdre, 'C'est Venus toute entière, à sa proie attachée,' or Hermione's lament: 'Errante et sans dessein, je cours dans ce palais'. Emotion rules the creatures of both Racine and Beaumont and Fletcher. But Beaumont and Fletcher's emotional situations with their alternating relaxation and tension, lack the volcanic intensity and concentration of those of the French dramatist. Phèdre's terrible agony is cumulative, that of Philaster and Arethusa cyclically heightened, dissipated, and renewed.

During Act IV their despair reaches its climax. The disillusioned Philaster, convinced of Arethusa's faithlessness, wanders alone in the forest and cries out in anguish:

> O that I had been nourished in these woods
> With Milk of Goats, and Acorns, and not known
> The right of Crowns nor the dissembling Trains
> Of womens looks; but dig'd my self a Cave
> Where I, my Fire, my Cattel, and my Bed
> Might have been shut together in one shed;

And then had taken me some Mountain Girl,
Beaten with Winds, chast as the hardened Rocks,
Whereon she dwells; that might have strewed my Bed
With leaves, and Reeds, and with the Skins of beasts
Our Neighbors; and have born at her big breasts
My large course issue. This had been a life
Free from vexation.

(IV, 1)

His naïve primitivism has the petulent adolescence of Tennyson's threat to 'Take a dusky woman, She shall bear my savage race'. Arethusa's state of mind is scarcely a more happy one. When the distracted Philaster comes upon her he can no longer contain himself. Finding her with Bellario, he takes out his sword and wounds her. As he does so, a country fellow bursts upon the scene.

Country Fellow: Hold, dastard, strike A Woman! th'art a craven I warrant thee, thou wouldst be loth to play half a dozen of venies at wasters with a good fellow for a broken head.

Philaster: Leave us good friend.

Arethusa: What ill bred man art thou, to intrude thyself upon our private sports, our recreations?

This short but revealing dialogue illustrates the peculiar emotional keying of much of the play. The country fellow (a woodcut in the first quarto depicts him as a rustic knight) suffers a chilly rebuke for his intrusion. George-A-Greene, the pattern of rustic Elizabethan chivalry, has no place in their world.

When the courtiers coming upon the scene discover the wounded Arethusa, she again rejects help, persistently crying, 'He has not hurt me . . . I felt it not'. Clearly we have wandered from the conventional paths of Elizabethan romance into the byways of love. Philaster and Arethusa anticipate the anguished delights of Otway's lovers or Liliom and Julie. Their love has an intensity and desperation, but it is at the same time strangely without meaning.

Philaster and Arethusa are as divorced from the world about them as they are from each other. In Shakespeare and in Molière we see man as an individual and as a member of society. But Philaster and Arethusa are isolated individuals in a disassociated society. Perhaps chiefly for this reason we feel in the tragi-comedies a sense of incoherency and disorder. Perhaps for this reason also their conversations so often seem like simultaneous monologues. Like the protagonists of heroic drama, each in his own hermetically sealed world, they have lost the capacity to communicate with each other.

Into this disordered world of tottering thrones, of distant alarums and excursions, of clashing absolutes, Beaumont and Fletcher introduce the types that dominate their subsequent tragi-comedies. Philaster sets the pattern for the vacillating hero. Arethusa, as virtuous as she is misunderstood, becomes the model for the long-suffering heroine. Bellario foreshadows a succession of Platonic lovers, and the king begets a long line of harsh tyrants. Megra and Pharamond, the lustful foils to Arethusa and Bellario, and Dion, the gruff, straight-speaking lord, complete the cast of characters that serve the authors so well.

The balance between the noble and the ignoble the playwrights preserve almost as carefully as they do in *The Faithful Shepherdess*. Both plays also show a markedly feminine accent. The authors invert the usual earlier triangle of two men and a woman. The hero suffers a noticeable feminization, and women and erotic situations increasingly dominate the action.

One can scarcely avoid seeing in this at least some reflections of the court of James I's reign, with its blurring and disordering of the older, conventional values. The Sicilian locale is patent subterfuge. Audiences and playwrights were only too aware of the affinities between Sicily and England.[4] The negotiations for the Spanish match in the opening scenes of the play prophetically mirror the similar later intrigues in James's court. Lustful relations between a lady and her page were only too conceivable in Whitehall, and one had not far to seek to find prototypes for Megra and Pharamond. (More than one commentator has drawn attention to the likeness between the scandalous Frances Howard and Evadne in *The Maid's Tragedy*.)

In such a world of intrigue and venality it is hard to find the measure of tragedy. Pity and terror do not thrive in these surroundings. Instead, the playwrights substitute for these emotions pathos and suspense—the staples of tragi-comedy. The fifth act may celebrate the triumph of Death or of Hymen. Death stands ready to enter at any one of the thousand doors always open to him, though the dramatists may contrive, at the last moment, to slam it in his face.

This emphasis on sensation constitutes both the strength and the weakness of Beaumont and Fletcher's tragi-comedy.

> It is like a ride on a roller coaster. It is breathless and exciting, and the whole technique is directed to keeping the roller coaster going through its dizzy swerves and plunges and recoveries, until the ride comes to a delicious end with everybody safe and sound and pleased with the fun—and it may be very good fun, if you happen to like it. Some people do not, and denounce it as a fraud or a menace; but this is not fair to the operators of the entertainment.[5]

In *The Maid's Tragedy* (c. 1610) Beaumont and Fletcher show an equal skill as entertainers within the more stringent limitations of tragedy. Played both at the court and at Blackfriars, it enjoyed frequent revivals before the closing of the theatres and after the Restoration. Of all the plays of the collaborators, it has perhaps had the most nearly unanimous praise from critics, with the notable exception of Thomas Rymer who, in a vigorous dissent, anatomized it as one of the most barbaric and artless tragedies of the previous age.[6] In the eyes of a neo-Aristotelian it is perhaps so. In another minority opinion Paul Elmer More found it an incomprehensible tangle of 'lust, love, loyalty and effrontery'.[7] On the other hand, John F. Danby finds it an archetype of Stuart drama.

The story of the play is not actually a complex one. At the king's request Amintor breaks his troth to Aspatia, the maid, and marries in her stead Evadne, sister to Melantius. On his wedding night Amintor discovers that his bride is in actuality the king's mistress, and his marriage one in name only. The next day he accosts Melantius and reveals to him his sister's shame. Melantius terrorizes his sister into repentance and Evadne, aghast at her sin, kills the lustful king. The lovelorn Aspatia, disguised as a page, provokes Amintor to kill her in combat, and, to complete the catalogue of deaths, Evadne and Amintor slay themselves.

The bare outlines of the plot would seem to qualify the authors for the accolade which Shaw bestowed upon Webster—'Tussaud Laureate'. But the play is devised with extraordinary skill. Retardation, surprise, contrast and irony—all of these masterfully intensify the action.

The opening of the first act is deliberately deceptive. Melantius returns from the wars to hear of Amintor's unexpected nuptials to Evadne. Aspatia, like a grief-stricken shadow, passes across the stage as the court gathers to celebrate the wedding. A nuptial masque begins, with Night rising in mists, followed by Cynthia, whose words ring with prophetic irony:

> Yet whil'st our raign lasts, let us stretch our power
> To give our servants one contented hour,
> With such unwonted solemn grace and state,
> As may forever after force them hate
> Our brothers glorious beams.
>
> (I, 1)

The action of the masque concludes to the rising wind and the raging sea. The pale East lightens as Evadne and Amintor prepare to retire to their marriage bed. The pomp of the feasting and the stormy Epithalamium of the masque contrast vividly with the pale, errant figure of Aspatia.

The second act parallels the first in its calculated use of juxtapositions. It opens with Evadne's ladies preparing her for the nuptial bed. Dula's immodest ribaldry shatters the brooding quiet of Evadne who asks her, 'Wilt take my place tonight?' a question which both Dula and the audience misconstrue. Aspatia bids goodnight to the lovers and, for the first time, Amintor begins to sense the extent of his wrong to her. He has betrayed her, though 'It was the king first moved me to't'. A premonition overcomes him—'Go not to bed'. His ensuing scene with Evadne, one of the finest in Beaumont and Fletcher, justifies the artifice and misdirection of the preceding ones. Amintor's passion meets with a frigid denial as Evadne bluntly informs him that she has sworn not to sleep with him. He attributes this to 'the coyness of a bride', but she stupefies him for the second time by telling him she detests him. Still unwilling to believe her, he interprets his as mere jesting.

Amintor: Leave and to bed.
If you have sworn to any of the Virgins
That were your old companions, to preserve
Your Maidenhead a night, it may be done
Without this means.
Evadne: A Maidenhead, *Amintor*,
At my years!

(II, I)

This time the shock is lasting, and it is brutally compounded.

I sooner will find out the beds of Snakes,
And with my youthful blood warm their cold flesh,
Letting them curl themselves about my limbs,
Than sleep one night with thee.

Only then is her virgin reluctance unmasked. Only then does she reveal the real reason for their marriage—to conceal her affair with the king. The impact of these discoveries and the impossibility of instantly avenging himself upon the sacred person of the king numb Amintor. Confronted by an apparently insoluble dilemma, he reaches an understanding with Evadne. Together they compact to feign a blissful marriage night.

Come, let us practice, and as wantonly
As ever loving Bride and Bridegroom met,
Lets laugh and enter here.

During the course of the scene Amintor and Evadne are both revealed in different lights. The lusting young bridegroom is seen, temporarily, as the disillusioned instrument of the king's convenience. The reluctant bride is exposed as the hardened, ambitious mistress of the king. The deliberate blinding of the audience in the preliminary scenes to the true nature of Evadne is justified by the theatricality of this one. The cumulative series of revelations which opens Amintor's eyes to the true nature of his bride and marriage has some of the jarring intensity of De Flores' terrible scene of self-revelation with Beatrice in Middleton's *The Changeling* (III, 4), but what is psychological exposure in Middleton is mere theatrical trickery in *The Maid's Tragedy*, albeit trickery of a high order. In Beaumont and Fletcher's scene the impact is less appalling, but nonetheless superbly effective through its alternately increasing and diminishing tensions concluding, not in a genuine emotional resolution, but on a note of irresolution, as Amintor and Evadne begin their bitter charade of a mock marriage.

The act draws to a close with a short scene, again in the best Beaumont and Fletcher vein, with the disconsolate Aspatia lamenting her fate and recounting to her ladies the legends of unhappy women. The abrupt entrance of Calianax, her father, interrupts the poignancy and quiet of the scene, and his harsh words, 'Up, you young lazy whores, up, or I'll swinge you,' bring the act to a close with a characteristic shift of mood and tempo.

The second most famous scene in the play, the quarrel between Melantius and Amintor in the ensuing act (III, 2), has been analyzed in great detail by Wallis to illustrate the dramaturgy of Beaumont and Fletcher.[8] Few question that for this scene they took as their model the quarrel between Brutus and Cassius. (Shakespeare's scene, with its shifting spectrum of emotions, appealed enormously to Dryden as well.) Though the Elizabethan drama is marked by its varied moods, this type of scene contrasts with the more usual Elizabethan technique of establishing a dominant mood within a scene, if not a play. The intrusion of the porter in *Macbeth* serves as the classic instance of deliberate disruption of mood, but in Beaumont and Fletcher prismatic shifts within the scene are the rule rather than the exception. In the quarrel scene between Melantius and Amintor the emotions of the men fluctuate violently, nonetheless the contrasts are organized and theatrically effective. The ordering of stimulus and response has been carefully calculated. But Beaumont and Fletcher are feeling not the pulse of their characters but of their audience. The psychology of the spectator governs the development of the scene into which the onlooker is drawn as irresistibly as he is into a baroque fresco of Tiepolo. Nonetheless, these engineered duologues make up many of the best scenes in Beaumont and Fletcher. (Dryden's later *Indian Emperor* and *Indian Queen* contain duologues and quartet scenes evolved with still greater, almost Euclidean, precision.)

The disparity between the real and the apparently real again serves as the occasion for a variety of dramatic effects. Thus, the seeming joy of Amintor and Evadne on the day after their marriage bewilders and angers the king, and in still another scene (IV, 2) the king's inability to distinguish the true from the false leads to the comic anguish of Calianax.

The two final acts contain a succession of highly theatrical scenes, but when the play ends, all passion spent, it is through sheer exhaustion rather than in genuine resolution. Little emerges from the welter of suffering and deaths. The individual scene is paramount, the totality far less impressive. The play concludes:

On lustful kings
Unlookt for sudden deaths from heaven are sent!
But curst is he that is their instrument.

The lines have, however, disappointingly limited application. They have no bearing on Evadne's transformation from an ambitious courtesan to a repentant wife. They do not relate to the complex experiences of Amintor and Aspatia.

Amintor has attempted to resolve an impossible dilemma. He is faced with the problem of killing the king, yet he cannot reconcile the doctrine of divine right to the necessity of keeping his own honour inviolate. The play demonstrates his growing awareness of the emptiness and irreconcilability of these concepts.

What a wild beast is uncollected man!
The thing that we call Honour, bears us all

Headlong unto sin, and yet itself is nothing.

(IV, 2)

The code of seventeenth century honour was often enough questioned. Falstaff epitomizes the comic jesting at its expense in his triumph over the dead Hotspur. Calderon's *Pintor de su Deshonra* concludes with a bitter commentary on the toll that honour exacts, and Corneille's *Le Cid* powerfully delineates its inexorable operation. Amintor wavers between acceptance and denial of its dictates, but the final bitter deadlock of two wills, that gives its compelling power to *Le Cid,* is impossible to the lost people of the world of Beaumont and Fletcher.

Aspatia's plight is no less tragic than Amintor's. As Danby interprets her, she stands for the traditional Elizabethan morality, the pure heroine of an earlier age, betrayed for the modern Jacobean heroine.[9] Like the later heroines of Ford, she seems powerless. Robbed of will, she moves through the play with the slow inevitability of a sleepwalker, and to her deeply moving scene with her maids (II, 2) Danby attaches a symbolic importance. As she contemplates a tapestry depicting the forsaken Ariadne, she sees in it the picture of her own fate.

I stand upon the Sea breach now, and think
Mine arms thus, and mine hair blown with the wind,
Wild as that desart; and let all about me
Tell that I am forsaken, do my face
(If thou hadst ever feeling of a sorrow)
Thus, thus, *Antiphila* strive to make me look
Like sorrows monument; and the trees about me
Let them be dry and leaveless; let the Rocks
Groan with continual surges, and behind me
Make all a desolation.

(II, 2)

She stands in a seventeenth century waste land. The emptiness and despair of this almost surrealist landscape foreshadow, perhaps, the wars and revolutions to come, the dessication of the Cavalier ideal. The poignancy of her words is real and touching, but it is at the same time unmistakably decadent. She takes melancholy pleasure in her self-projection into the company of deserted women—Dido, Ariadne and Oenone. The emotion, as usual in Beaumont and Fletcher, is anticipated, not experienced. Her lines quoted above, if they symbolize the despair of the age, have also the self-consciousness of Marvell's directions to a painter.

An earlier scene demonstrates this same persistent posturing. In her farewell to Evadne she remarks:

> May no discontent
> Grow, 'twixt your Love and you; but if there do,
> Enquire of me, and I will guide your moan,
> Teach you an artificial way to grieve,
> To keep your sorrow waking; love your Lord
> No worse than I; but if you love so well,
> Alas, you may displease him, so did I.
> This is the last time you shall look on me:
> Ladies, farewell; as soon as I am dead,
> Come all and watch one night about my Hearse;
> Bring each a mournful story and a tear
> To offer at it when I go to earth:
> With flattering Ivie clasp my Coffin round,
> Write on my brow my fortune, let my Bier
> Be born by Virgins that shall sing by course
> The truth of maids and perjuries of men.
>
> (II, 1)

One cannot deny the emotional effectiveness of this passage which has the baroque heightening of Bernini's St. Theresa or Beata Ludovica Albertoni, with the calculated drama of their attitudes, the artfully disposed marble folds of their dress. More than half in love with easeful death, Aspatia busies herself devising a tableau in which she can appear to advantage. 'Teach you an artificial way to grieve,' is her way of expressing it. The sensuous melancholy of her lines contrasts vividly with, for example, Juliet's agonized vision of death (IV, 3). Aspatia's grief is genuine, but its profundity is open to question. Dr. Johnson's historic doubts on the validity of Milton's lament for *Lycidas* ('Where there is leisure for fiction there is little grief') apply even more aptly to Aspatia's preoccupation with the accessories of sorrow.

The concluding scene of the play illustrates the same high theatricality and questionable tragic conception. Amintor dies, flanked by the bodies of Evadne and Aspatia. Behind them, as Henry Wells has pointed out, stand a formal trio of mourners: Melantius, behind his friend, Amintor; Calianax, behind his daughter, Aspatia; Diphilus, apparently created for this occasion, behind the body of his sister, Evadne.[10] Such scenes have a real impact in the theatre. On the page they tend to pass unnoticed or to seem like mere groupings of window dummies. In such artifice Beaumont and Fletcher excel, but at the cost of continuity of plot and psychology. Between the concluding couplets of one scene and the opening lines of another, characters make sudden resolves; the lost is found; the disguise is assumed or cast off. The *scène à faire* lies buried in the hiatus between as the dramatists busily regroup and rearrange. In place of orderly gradations of plot and character they offer a series of striking tableaux. But rarely are we permitted to look backstage, to see the transitions, the shifting from one attitude to another.

A King and No King shares the merits and demerits of *Philaster* but in spirit comes closest to the Fletcherian definition of tragicomedy. It had a brilliant reception when in 1611 the King's Men performed it at the court, Blackfriars, and the Globe, and it enjoyed frequent revivals during the remainder of the century. Rymer, as one might expect, blasted it, but Dryden singled it out for praise in the *Essay on Dramatic Poesie*, and as recent a critic as Arthur Mizener shares his admiration for the management of the plot.[11] By and large, however, our obsession with dramatic psychology blinds us to such virtuoso plot-making, and Aristotle's emphasis on plot confronts us with an uncomfortable critical heresy which did not exist for seventeenth-century spectators and readers who were far readier than we are to accept the artifice of a well-wrought story.

Attributed largely to Beaumont, with Fletcher generally credited with the story outline, the management of the comedy, and the mob scene, *A King and No King* has a highly contrived premise. Acting on a generous impulse, Arbaces, king of Armenia, offers the hand of his sister, Panthea, whom he has not seen for many years, to his defeated rival, Tigranes. The first obstacle to the match develops when Spaconia, herself in love with Tigranes, successfully pleads with Panthea not to marry him. The second deterrent is of a more serious nature. When Arbaces finally confronts his sister, he falls violently and hopelessly in love with her. At this point the play really begins. The characters have been manoeuvred into place, and only if we grant the extraordinary *donnée* can we relish the skill with which the authors develop this situation.

For their success in doing so they depend on the devices so strikingly exploited before: contrasts of character, surprise, emotional reversals within a scene, prolongation and retardation—all centering, as Arthur Mizener points out, on 'emotional rather than narrative climaxes'. Throughout, the play abounds with those tricks of suspense so dear to Fletcher's disciple, Massinger. But the collaborators make sure to provide us with carefully interpolated clues. The riddling title contains the key to the puzzle, as does Mardonius' remark: 'Were you not the king, from amongst men I should/Have chosen you out to love among the rest'. Gobrias' warning against hastily marrying off the unseen Panthea, and Arbaces' instinctive disbelief in his relation to Panthea—''Tis false!' must similarly have alerted the wary. Instinctively Beaumont and Fletcher adopted de Vega's technique:

> In the first act set for the case. In the second weave together the events, in such wise that until the middle of the third act one may hardly guess the outcome. Always trick expectancy . . . [12]

Nonetheless the clues are there, and spectators who loved the tale for the tale's sake doubtless did not let them slip by unnoticed. Their deep draughts of Boccaccio and Painter prepared them for such tales of trickery. They could witness Helena's conquest of Bertram in *All's Well That Ends Well* without deeply pondering whether in so doing she laid the foundation for a happy marriage. They had much of the pleasure in artful story-telling that some readers find today in the well-laid mystification of detective fiction. But one can legitimately question whether such artifice does not seriously impair the tragic impact of such a subject as incestuous love, and where Ford in *'Tis Pity She's a Whore* leads us over the precipice of tragedy, Beaumont and Fletcher in *A King and No King* lead us merely to the brink.

The opening scenes of the play are characteristically misleading. Arbaces, as we first see him, seems scarcely more than a tyrant-buffoon. But his sudden and tragic love changes the nature of the play and exposes an unrevealed depth in his personality. The portrait of him which emerges has a fullness and dimension that Beaumont and Fletcher rarely achieve elsewhere. Arbaces is both generous and corrupt, noble and cowardly, wise and foolish. Two antithetical scenes and characters reveal the dichotomy in him. In the first of these he avows his unlawful passion for Panthea to Mardonius, his forthright friend and counsellor.

> I would desire her love
> Lasciviously, lewdly, incestuously,
> To do a sin that needs must damn us both,
> And thee too . . .
>
> (III, 3)

The brutal admission horrifies the good old man. Mardonius' shock in turn sobers Arbaces into repentance, but the appearance of Bessus, the cowardly courtier and comic counterpart of Arbaces, rekindles his hopes of enjoying Panthea. Once again the playwrights make use of a reversal. The eagerness of Bessus to serve as the king's pander leads him to suggest: 'If you have a mind to your Mother, tell me, and you shall see I'le set it hard.' The gross carnality of this suggestion shocks even Arbaces, and the act concludes with the king's firm resolve to stifle his love.

This dramatic description of Arbaces' anguish illustrates the Beaumont and Fletcher technique of tension and relaxation almost perfectly. The scene between the king and Panthea (IV, 4) also demonstrates this pulsation and contrived surprise. Arbaces' declaration that he has lost 'The only difference betwixt man and beast, My reason' meets with Panthea's unlooked-for admission that she shares his emotion. Quite unexpectedly she declares her love, and the scene concludes on a deliberately suggestive note as she rebukes, 'Methinks brothers and sisters lawfully may kiss'.

Tigranes also endures love's martyrdom in his inability to choose between Spaconia and Panthea, but the incestuous love of Arbaces and Panthea eclipses all the other elements of the play. Fantastic as the initial premise may be, vague as the play's Armenian setting may be, the emotion which overpowers them is all too real. In the grip of this emotion they themselves become real. They belong neither among the semi-allegorical figures of *The Faithful Shepherdess* nor among the eccentric humourists of *Cupid's Revenge* and *The Woman Hater*. The intensity and reality of their emotion separates them from the other inhabitants of the world of tragi-comedy. In short, during the course of the play they come to life, to become mere manikins again in the Gilbertian, Little Buttercup resolution of the fifth act.

A King and No King, as Waith indicates, marks the crystallization of the pattern of tragi-comedy. Its action transpires in a world both recognizably real and yet remote; its plot and construction show marked contriving; its characters are Protean; both 'ease and rhetorical formality' stamp its language. As a dramatic *genre* with stringent limitations, appeal to a specific audience, narrowness of theme, and generally restricted *dramatis personae*, it points forward to the heroic drama of the aristocratic Restoration audience.

Unfortunately many problems becloud Beaumont and Fletcher's comedies of collaboration. Many of these were not published until the 1647 Folio, by which time they had undergone revision by Massinger, Rowley and others. Two comedies casually referred to in Beaumont's verse letter to Ben Jonson as written in collaboration during a country sojourn, Beaumont did not even take the trouble to name. Many an earnest critic, intent on establishing these niceties in the Beaumont and Fletcher canon, has been swallowed up in the quicksands of speculation and debate.

One might hazard the guess, however, that *The Coxcomb* constitutes one of the country recreations of the two young men, particularly in view of its rustic sub-plot. Perhaps, indeed, the play antedates both *Cupid's Revenge* and *Philaster*, since we know that it had been performed at least two years before its 1612 production by the Children of the Queen's Revels. Though condemned in its original version as too long, it was 'well received by men of worth' both at this time and during the subsequent revivals before 1636 and after 1682.

In this comedy the mixed moods of tragi-comedy prevail. The comedy of the man-who-would-be-cuckold (usually considered the work of Fletcher) clashes with the romantic subplot, the love of Viola and Ricardo (generally attributed to Beaumont). Undeniably the two stories fit awkwardly together. Fletcher's comic creation, Antonio, cannot artistically accommodate himself into Beaumont's world, with its strong reminiscences of Shakespeare's *Twelfth Night:*

> Peace, fair *Viola?*
> Fair *Viola?* Who should have left her here
> On such a ground? If you had meant to lose her,
> You might have found there were no ecchos here
> To take her name, and carry it about,
> When her true lover came to mourn for her,
> Till all the neighboring valleys and the hills,
> Resounded *Viola*.
>
> (V, 1)

Shakespeare's Illyria has the romantic scope to contain both the robust comedy of Sir Toby and the poignant anguish of Viola. *The Coxcomb* has no such breadth of conception or unifying tone, though Fletcher in his later collaborations did succeed in wedding lively satire to romantic pathos.

His contribution tells the story of Antonio, his wife Maria, and his friend Mercury. On discovering Mercury's interest in Maria, the excessively generous Antonio insists on helping to gratify his friend's desires. Maria's outraged protests have no effect. Antonio even adopts the expedient of disguise to help satisfy Mercury's wish to cuckold him. The story ends on a curious note. Maria's simulated lust finally cures Mercury's passion for her, but Antonio, consistent to the last, apologizes for his wife's obstinate virtue. The cynicism and carefree sexuality of this plot have offended many. The theme is scarcely an attractive one, nor have the characters much appeal, though Antonio in his disguise as an Irishman occasionally displays irresistible, high-spirited humour.

The parallels to Dekker's *Honest Whore* (1604) give some substance to Gayley's argument that *The Coxcomb* was written before 1608. In Dekker's play Candido, an over-complaisant draper, so demoralizes his wife that as a final expedient she tries to shock him into sanity—i.e. normal male aggressiveness—by having him confined to Bedlam. Neither of these stories of patient male Griseldas fits comfortably into modern categories of humour. But of the two, Fletcher's is by far the more awkward, with neither the robust quality of Dekker nor the bitter impact of Cervantes' tragic tale of a chastity test, *El Curioso Impertinente* sometimes cited as Fletcher's source.

Beaumont's subplot, the romance of Ricardo and Viola, has far more interest. Separated from her lover and unrecognized by him during a midnight brawl, Viola flees into the countryside. There she begins an unhappy odyssey that recalls Breton's *Miseries of Mavillia*. A tinker and his trull rob her. A country gentleman offers to help her but makes his purpose in doing so clearly apparent. Befriended at last by Nan and Madge, two milkmaids, Viola cries out gratefully:

> What true contented happiness dwels here
> More than in Cities! Wou'd to God my Father
> Had liv'd like one of these, and bred me up
> To milk: and do as they do: methinks
> 'Tis a life that I wou'd choose, if I were now
> To tell my time agen, above a Princes.
>
> (III, 1)

Her cry echoes Philaster's apostrophe to the simple life, but here Beaumont explores its rich comic possibilities. Mercury's mother, a countrywoman, hires her as a servant—with disastrous results. Viola breaks a glass and overturns the sweet-meats, to the vigorous displeasure of the old lady. So might Marie Antoinette have fared had she abandoned the delights of the *hameau* to seek employment as a real shepherdess.

During these country episodes Beaumont's dialogue moves effortlessly from verse to prose and back to verse again. The sharp-tongue, pungent diatribes of Mercury's mother, and the good-humoured prose of Nan and Madge, as colloquial as their names, alternate with the quiet wistful verse of Viola. The freshness, the purity and the poetry which she brings to the play contrast vividly with the coltish energy of the Tom Jones-like Ricardo and the vigorous realism of the scenes in which he appears. The drinking scene between Ricardo and his friends, and the thumbnail portraits of the tinker and his trull have the authenticity of miniatures in the Luttrell Psalter. Viola is scarcely more at home in this world than Euphrasia in the corrupt courts of Sicily, but *The Coxcomb* is, after all, a comedy, and Beaumont permits Viola the luxury of a happy reconciliation with Ricardo. As her lover kneels before her, begging her forgiveness for the unhappiness he has caused her, she tells him:

> I have made a story,
> Will serve to waste many a winters fire
> When we are old, I'll [tell] my daughters then
> The miseries their Mother had in love.
>
> (V, I)

As a heroine Viola is sometimes worthy to stand beside her Shakespearian namesake.

The remaining comedies in which Beaumont and Fletcher probably collaborated have less interest and pose many questions. It is as hard to date them as to determine the playwrights' respective shares. Almost certainly *Wit at Several Weapons* (1609?) belongs largely to Middleton. The lively vernacular prose of this comedy of contemporary London life, with its gulling and knavery, its lampooning of humour types, inevitably calls to mind such a work as *A Trick to Catch the Old One*, though it anticipates also Fletcher's *Monsieur Thomas*. Sir Perfidious Oldcraft, a passionate admirer of wit, suspects Wittypate, his son, of insufficient endowment in this respect. His consequent disgust, and the desperation of his son, threatened with disinheritance for his stupidity, set off a complicated train of intrigues. Plots and counterplots follow each other in chain reaction until Wittypate can prove himself the true possessor of wit.

The amorous imbroglios of the plot and the emphasis on wit suggest some aspects of later comedy, but only remotely so. We remain closer to the Jonsonian pattern of the duper and the duped than to the Restoration comedy of manners. *Wit At Several Weapons* calls to mind the first unpolished phase of Restoration comedy, Etherege's *Love in a Tub* rather than the exquisite comedy of Congreve. On the surface *Wit At Several Weapons* has several points in common with *The Way of the World*. 'An old doating croane,' her niece Mirabell, and Cunningham, who courts the old lady to insure access to her niece, while vaguely parallel to Lady Wishfort, Millamant and Mirabell, seem like the roughest of cartoons beside Congreve's finished portraits. The foolery of *Wit At Several Weapons* seems like horseplay in contrast to the elegant charades of *The Way of the World*, and Sir Perfidious Oldcraft, great a connoisseur of wit as he was, would infinitely have preferred Jonson's Mosca to Congreve's Mirabell.

The Scornful Lady (c. 1613), a far better comedy, remains one of the happiest experiments of Beaumont and Fletcher in this *genre*. Probably originally written for the Children of the Queen's Revels at Blackfriars, it underwent subsequent revisions by Fletcher for the King's Men. The opening scene and the close of the play most critics attribute to Beaumont, with the central intrigues largely Fletcher's invention. The seven quartos which appeared before the 1679 Folio attest to its great success, and its history upon the stage refutes the sour verdict of Gayley: 'If this is the best of which they were capable in that kind, it is as well that they did not produce more.'[13]

Also a prose comedy of contemporary society, in most respects it betters *Wit at Several Weapons*. Its boisterous laughter and high spirits even lend it the illusion of real wit, but, to paraphrase Congreve's observation of the comedy of Cibber, *The Scornful Lady* has the *sound* of wit rather than its substance. Nonetheless, the sheer buoyancy of the play carries the reader along, and in stage terms it offers real opportunities for actors. (The characterization of Savil, the perfect English butler, is one of Fletcher's minor masterpieces, and his alteration from rigid disapproval of his master's high living to joyous participation makes one of Fletcher's happiest comic turnabouts.)

Two neatly intersecting triangles make up its design. Elder Loveless and Welford vie for the favours of The Lady; Young Loveless and Morecraft, the usurer, compete for the hand of a rich young widow. The sex duel that animates the first group points forward to the sex opposition of the Restoration: 'I had rather die, sometimes, than not disagree in public with him who people think I love.' The most brilliantly amusing scenes in the play belong to III and IV with their amorous fencing and comic peripeteia. As in the tragi-comedies, much hinges on the reversals of emotion and situation, so in these scenes the advantage shifts from one reluctant lover to another. Mock deaths, mock avowals, mock protestations ensue before the scornful lady can be purged of her humour: 'To love being absent, and when he's [present] laugh at him and abuse him.'

The underplot of the taming of the prodigal, Young Loveless, offers parallels to the main one, and its sex-intrigues also suggest that later staple of comedy, the sex-chase. But Young Loveless and his roistering friends although they share with the professional cuckolders of the Restoration a zest for the chase, have little of their social or verbal dexterity. As The Lady remarks: 'This room was built for honest meaners, that deliver themselves hastily and plainly, and are gone. Is this a time or place for *Exordiums*, and *Similes* and *Metaphors*?' The murmurs of the alcovistes in the salons of the Marquise de Rambouillet had not yet reached England. Fletcher's dialogue has instead the coarse, vigorous fibre of Jacobean conversation. His characters and situations as well, although drawn from classical comedy, he has completely Anglicized. The play breathes with the spirit of seventeenth century London, with its Massinger-like awareness of Jacobean manners and moneys.

The two remaining comedies possibly of joint authorship warrant little attention. In all likelihood the King's Men played both *The Captain* (c. 1612) and *The Nice Valour* (c. 1615–25). Both remained unpublished until the 1647 Folio and their rawness and

D

unsuccessful blending of ingredients suggest a relationship to the early satirical humour comedy, *The Woman Hater*. *The Captain* in particular echoes the earlier play and contains virtually every defect for which critics have assailed Fletcher. Its misogyny is marked by unusual coarseness and virulence. In part, at least, Captain Jacomo's aversion to the sex has its justification. Few characters in the Beaumont and Fletcher canon can match Lelia in sheer distastefulness. She outdoes the Scornful Lady in devising torments for her lovers. She denies her father charity. When he appears disguised, she courts him amorously, and even after he reveals his identity she persists in her lustful solicitations. In addition to this erotic and incestuous scene we find still another episode exploring homosexuality and others dedicated to scatological humour.

As Alfred Harbage has pointed out, such scenes mark the work of the coterie playwrights, and recur with particular frequency in the work of John Marston, who contributed so much to setting the tone of the Beaumont and Fletcher comedies. *The Captain* shows this influence strongly. The relationship of Julio-Angelo-Lelia with its mingling of satiric and romantic overtones calls to mind Freevil and Malheureux' infatuation for the Dutch Courtezan, with whom Lelia has much in common. Both plays share a moral ambivalency. One cannot draw with any surety the line of demarcation between satire and pornography. Lelia's final promise to reform is cynical and perfunctory, and as a creation she fails, for we are invited to consider her both as a satirical portrait of a lecherous woman and also as a romantic heroine.

The Nice Valour adds little more lustre to the canon. The lack of names for the characters, the confusion between them, the complicated parallel action, and the strings of execrable puns all mar a play which has few compensating virtues. Its plotting has, however, some interest, and its general design far more purpose than at first seems evident. Two concepts, 'honour' and 'gentility' weld the play together and in a series of laboratory demonstrations the *dramatis personae* illustrate their definition. A light touch with a switch triggers Shamont's Castilian sense of honour and inflames his desire for revenge upon the king who has offered him this affront. Shamont's brother's honour suffers a blemish when a gang of hired ruffians attack him. The cowardly Lapet, at the other end of the scale, gladly endures insults and calls the whole code of honour into question by meditating 'what honour a man may lose by a kick'. Similarly the play repeatedly examined the concept of 'gentility', and in the last scene the Duke's eyes are opened to the fact that a 'gentleman' cannot be created.

If, as Maxwell argues, the play can be dated between 1615-1616, Beaumont can have had little or no hand in it.[14] Certainly in many respects the play suggests the court life of that period. The theme of 'gentility' may well have bearing on James's wholesale creation of titles, and the Duke's obsession with Shamont inevitably calls to mind the rise of James's favourite, Villiers. The Duke and James I share a number of traits—a passion for the hunt, the divine gift of healing, a preference for a womanless court, and an absolutist outlook. There the parallelism ends, and there perhaps it should end. One had, after all, to be diplomatic.

Artistically the play fails, as *The Captain* does, through its failure to achieve any kind of unified effect. The parallel plots of Shamont and Lapet, one serious and one comic, never properly fuse. The play suffers also from a tone even more markedly unpleasant than that of *The Captain*. Lapet's cowardice passes beyond the limits of slapstick into pathology. So willing is he to endure affronts that he has compiled a comic handbook of which Sacher-Masoch might have approved—*The Uprising of the Kick and the Downfall of the Duello*. His conversation with the Clown in Act III, a comparison of injuries and affronts received, evokes the uneasy laughter of the Barabas-Ithamore interview in the *Jew of Malta*. The Madman in *The Nice Valour* also has curious tastes. He is 'allowed a carcass to insult on—' and participates in a comic homosexual wooing scene. The Madman's beloved adds a final grotesque note to the play. Although in an advanced stage of pregnancy, she elects to come upon the scene disguised as Cupid. The sum total of these elements adds up to a play of almost uniquely disagreeable atmosphere.

That the majority of the comic collaborations of Beaumont and Fletcher should have failed can occasion little surprise. Even a generation of strong-stomached playgoers must, on occasion, have found them guilty of exploiting questionable sources of laughter. They had discarded the humours of Chapman and Ben Jonson in favour of more sensational ones. Following in the footsteps of Marston, they too often made use of the *recherché* or the pornographic, disguised under the thin veneer of morality. Yet one cannot say that the comedies are without fun. Whatever their moral ambiguity, their uneasy yoking of the serious and the comic, these plays are for the stage. Almost always one senses the opportunities for stage business, and the easy accommodation of the speech to the actor's mouth.

Shaw's grudging admission to 'a condescending tolerance for Beaumont and Fletcher' shows at least a reluctant professional admiration for them as men of the theatre. Quite correctly Shaw finds in them 'no depth, no conviction, no religious or philosophical basis, no real power or seriousness'.[15] One can hardly dispute the meretricious design and appeal of their comedies, but the great master of paradox and criticism might have expanded his remarks and uncovered an interesting critical paradox.

The shallowness, the muddied morality which mar most of the comedies, make up the essential background of their tragicomedies. The world of *The Nice Valour* with its debates on 'honour' and 'gentility', its warped concepts of love, its cynical view of kingship, is essentially that of *The Maid's Tragedy*, but it is a world whose disorder lends itself to tragi-comedy rather than to comedy. An age of absolutism, the Jacobean period was also an age of scepticism. In tragi-comedy this clash found its expression. But it was not after all a purely Jacobean phenomenon. La Fontaine's advice: 'Quant à vous, suivez Mars, ou l'Amour, ou le Prince,'[16] summarized the dilemma of the Cavalier Age.

NOTES TO CHAPTER TWO

1. Gerald Eames Bentley, 'Shakespeare and the Blackfriars Theatre', *Shakespeare Survey* (I), Cambridge University Press, 1948, pp. 38–50.
2. Sir John Harington, *Nugae Antiquae*, London, 1804, I, p. 352.
3. John F. Danby, *Poets on Fortune's Hill*, London, 1952, pp. 162–177.
4. See, for example, Massinger's *Maid Of Honour*, I, 1.
5. Harold S. Wilson, '*Philaster* and *Cymbeline*', *English Institute Essays* (1951), New York, 1952, pp. 163–164.

6. Thomas Rymer, *The Tragedies of the Last Age Considered*, London, 1678, pp. 104–139.
7. Paul Elmer More, 'Beaumont and Fletcher' (I), *The Nation*, April 24, 1913, p. 410.
8. Lawrence B. Wallis, *Fletcher, Beaumont and Company*, New York, 1947, pp. 220–228.
9. Danby, *Poets on Fortune's Hill*, pp. 184–206.
10. Henry W. Wells, *Elizabethan and Jacobean Playwrights*, New York, 1939, pp. 124–127.
11. Arthur Mizener, 'The High Design of *A King and No King*', *Modern Philology*, XXXVIII (1940), pp. 133–154.
12. Lope De Vega, *Arte Nuevo . . .* (1609) quoted in Barrett Clark, *European Theories of the Drama*, New York, 1947, p. 92.
13. Charles M. Gayley, *Beaumont, the Dramatist*, New York, 1914, p. 376.
14. Baldwin Maxwell, *Studies in Beaumont, Fletcher and Massinger*, Chapel Hill, University of North Carolina Press, 1939, pp. 116–137.
15. George Bernard Shaw, *Plays and Players*, Oxford University Press, 1952, pp. 307–309.
16. *Fables:* 'Le Meunier, Son Fils et l'Âne'.

THREE

FLETCHER'S UNAIDED WORK

HOWEVER much they may disagree in assessing the work of John Fletcher, his critics almost unanimously agree that he had little talent for tragedy. 'No man can have formed a just idea of possible *tragic* drama, as opposed to possible *comic* drama, and not find in this tragedy of *Valentinian* a convincing proof that the writer was utterly incapable of tragedy,' wrote Coleridge.[1] Critics as divergent as Miss Orie Hatcher and Rupert Brooke concur in finding Fletcher's talents, often so effective in comedy or tragi-comedy, ill-suited to more serious drama. In all likelihood Fletcher would have agreed with them. He wrote no more than two independent tragedies, The dark muse hardly appealed to him as much as her comic sister, or half-sister, tragi-comedy.

Both *Bonduca* and *Valentinian* belonged to the repertory of The King's Men and can be dated between the years 1609–1614. Neither enjoyed a conspicuous success, though subsequent revisions by Rochester and George Powell prolonged their stage life, and *Bonduca* continued to have occasional performances until the nineteenth century. Actually, neither play fits comfortably into any conventional category of tragedy, and one suspects that even the liberal-minded Jacobean audiences found them peculiar.

As a source for the first play Fletcher turned to Holinshed, that much-worked mine of historical dramas. Though fashionable audiences had wearied of the drum and trumpet chronicles so popular before the turn of the century, Holinshed offered playwrights an unexhausted vein of riches of still another kind in English mytho-history. Upon this rich lode Shakespeare drew twice in *King Lear* and in *Cymbeline*. The latter play, in particular, has an interesting, if speculative, relationship to Fletcher's play. *Bonduca* may have been written either before or immediately after Shakespeare's work. The list of the principal actors in Fletcher's play indicates its production between 1609–1611 or 1613–1614. The latter date seems more probable, however, as Baldwin Maxwell has pointed out.[2] The humours of the hungry knave, Judas, whose leanness provides a running joke, suggest that the appropriately-named John Shanke played this part around 1614. Fletcher's usual method of appropriating Shakespearian material and inverting it further strengthens the argument for a later date. It is quite in keeping with Fletcher's habit that if in *Cymbeline* Shakespeare gives us a drama of a legendary English king, in *Bonduca* Fletcher should give us that of a legendary English queen.

Internal evidence also argues a date of composition later than 1609. One of the most appealing features of *Bonduca* lies in the characterization of Hengo, 'a brave boy'. His relationship to Caratach, a hardened old soldier, stands out as the most sympathetically delineated in the play. (Bonduca has scarcely more importance than Cymbeline.) The fifth act of the play belongs almost exclusively to Caratach and Hengo, and the death scene of the young boy Swinburne acclaimed as one of the peaks of English drama. The note struck is a pathetic one, of the sort Fletcher sounds so effectively in the tragi-comedies. Hengo, after bravely defending himself against a crowd of cowardly Roman bullies, is treacherously slain by the contemptible Judas. Caratach, in revenge, kills the Roman with a stone, and, as the young Hengo dies in his arms, he laments:

> Farewel the hopes of *Britain*,
> Thou Royal graft, Farewel for ever. Time and Death,
> Ye have done your worst. Fortune now see, now proudly
> Pluck off thy vail, and view thy triumph: Look
> Look what thou hast brought this Land to. Oh fair flower,
> How lovely yet thy ruines show, how sweetly
> Even death embraces thee! The peace of heaven,
> The fellowship of all great souls be with thee.
>
> (V, 3)

One can scarcely forbear italicizing 'yet'. If the lines make up a graceful elegy for a valiant young Briton, they suggest as well an appropriate tribute to young Prince Henry, James's heir, and the hope of England, who had succumbed to typhoid fever in 1612 at the age of eighteen. The young prince, totally unlike both his father and his lame, sickly, younger brother, Charles, had seemed to promise a return to a more chivalric age. He detested the favourite Carr; he had even set himself against his father by courting the friendship of Sir Walter Raleigh, then a political prisoner in the Tower. Those who hated James for his cautious and pacific policies, had found a hero in the young prince. They felt an admiration also for Raleigh. The great Elizabethan worthy could not accommodate himself to the Jacobean regime. His vigour and impetuousness, which even Elizabeth at times found embarrassing, appeared downright intolerable to her successor.

One hesitates to make a *pièce à clef* of *Bonduca* by suggesting that Fletcher intended Caratach as a portrait of Raleigh, but the gruff, independently-minded protector of Hengo has at least some features in common with him. Admittedly, both *Valentinian* and *The Loyal Subject* expose one to the same temptation, though to a lesser degree. In the former play, the honest old soldier, Aecius, contrasts vividly with the bawds and parasites of Valentinian's court; in the latter, the loyal counsellor, Archas, stands out in bold relief against the corrupt entourage of the king. Caratach is not a highly individual characterization, but neither does he belong completely to a type. We can hardly fail to sense through him the sympathy which Fletcher expresses for the political malcontents of James's reign. Certainly the author cannot be accused, as he has been, of 'servile cowering' before the doctrine of Stuart absolutism.

As Eugene Waith has pointed out, *Bonduca* has many of the characteristics of tragi-comedy. At the same time, it anticipates various features of heroic drama. In the opening scene Bonduca, the virago queen, exhorts her troops to battle with the shrill vigour of Davenant's Roxolana. But during this scene, largely a duologue with Caratach, her general, she makes a *volte-face* of the type we associate with tragi-comedy. Her anger subsides. Under the impact of Caratach's measured words her scornful mockery of the Romans dwindles to a more sober attitude.

Thy temperance has cur'd that Tympany,

And given me health again, nay, more discretion.
Shall we have peace? for now I love these *Romans*.
(I, 1)

The second scene also combines tragi-comic and heroic elements. Junius, captain of the Romans, falls in love with one of Bonduca's daughters, and the fate of Britain hangs in the balance as he tries to reconcile the conflicting demands of love and honour. For four acts Fletcher keeps the outcome in suspense. He mixes spectacle, low comedy and love scenes, and a succession of plots and counterplots, stratagems and reversals keeps the plot spinning. Even the last scene, in the manner of tragi-comedy, has its changes of fortune.

Though the final death toll might justify calling this play a 'tragedy', little else does. Like *Valentinian,* it fits awkwardly into any conventional category of tragedy. This difficulty Charles Gayley noted in commenting on these two plays:

> They involve moral conduct, to be sure, patriotism, loyalty, chivalry, military prowess, insane lust, and vengeance, but they lack deep-seated and deliberate motive of action, and they fail of that inevitability of spiritual conflict which is requisite to tragic effect.[3]

Of the 'inevitability' that Gayley seeks there is none. A 'deliberate motive of action' proves as elusive. The impulse in *Bonduca* (as in Shakespeare's *Troilus and Cressida*) is centrifugal. The energy in Fletcher's play dissipates itself in a host of directions. Bonduca serves merely as the mouthpiece for passionate declamation. Only the figures of the old soldier and the young Hengo emerge with sufficiently life-like dimension and purpose to lend the play some substance of tragic consequence and to differentiate it from the mass of sensational tragi-comedies of Fletcher and his collaborators.

Valentinian exhibits many of these same flaws, but as Lawrence Wallis has demonstrated, this tragedy of rape and revenge Fletcher has constructed far more carefully.[4] Each act centres on a minor and major crisis. At the end of each act he leaves the audience with a question in its mind. Will Valentinian ravish Lucina? What revenge, if any, will her husband, Maximus, take? And so on. But Fletcher once again pays the price for the sacrifice of tragic inevitability to suspense. We are far more interested in the action than in its causation or meaning.

The central dilemma strongly resembles that of *The Maid's Tragedy*. How is Maximus to reconcile the avenging of his wife's rape by the emperor with an attack upon his sovereign person? Through a debate the author weighs the possible courses of action, but he is characteristically unable to face this dilemma squarely. Through its revenge theme it relates to the nearly contemporary *The Atheist's Tragedy* (1607–11) and *The Revenge of Bussy D'Ambois* (1607–12). Fletcher fails, however, to take Tourneur's and Chapman's clear-cut moral position. As Bowers has noted in his study of the revenge tragedy, the increasing Christianization of tragedy had by this time brought about fundamental changes in this *genre*.[5] The demand for 'an eye for an eye' had given way to a more Christian doctrine of passive forbearance. Charlemont and Clermont stand for the new order of Christian avenger, content to await the operation of heaven's justice. In Fletcher's play the problem of revenge or forbearance also arises. Considerations not of Christianity, but of the doctrine of divine right, cause Maximus to hesitate to avenge his wife's dishonour. As he debates the problem with his friend Aecius, the problem seems to admit no solution. When Maximus retires from the scene he has not yet decided upon a course of action. When he returns he has made up his mind to avenge himself upon Valentinian. Apparently Fletcher has resolved the dilemma. Actually he has not done so, for at this point he provides Maximus with a fresh motivation quite unconnected with his desire to avenge his wife's rape. He metamorphoses Maximus into an unscrupulous politician who uses his wife's rape as the excuse to bring about, through wily indirection, the emperor's death by poison. The sympathetic revenger gives way to the self-seeking revenger. The moral dilemma has been muddied and Fletcher has managed to avoid resolving the clash between the doctrine of divine right and the demands of honour. Maximus, turned Machiavellian, decides to seize the throne for himself. 'If I rise, my wife was ravished well,' he declares as he unabashedly and hypocritically woos the elderly empress Eudoxia. In the last scene, his ambitions apparently satisfied, he prepares to ascend the throne, but the coronation, in the literal Fletcherian manner, proves his undoing. The empress crowns him with a poisoned wreath and, as he dies, she justifies herself by accusing him of responsibility for the deaths of both Aecius and Valentinian. Her words excite the Roman mob to rapturous applause.

> Romans, she is righteous,
> And such a piece of justice Heaven must smile on.
>
> (V, 8)

The effect is wry and ironic. Sinner and revenger stand on the same plane. The initial rape of Lucina has been forgotten, and through a sudden twist in the last act Valentinian becomes a royal martyr. Again this is a decentralized play. It begins as the tragedy of Lucina, continues as the tragedy of Maximus, and concludes as the tragedy of Valentinian, as Fletcher throws his sympathy first one way then another.

But the effect is not tragic. Fletcher's sudden sleights-of-hand and reversals prevent him from achieving either tragedy or melodrama. Instead, he gives us a series of disassociated scenes of sensation.

Seen in this light, *Valentinian* can be called a success. The play has an operatic intensity and shrillness to it, though Fletcher sometimes achieves his most telling effects through the simplest means and language. There is a terrible, crushing finality, reminiscent of James's own manner of speech, in the words of Valentinian as the ravished Lucina confronts him.

> *Lucina:* As long as there is motion in my body,
> And life to give me words, I'le cry for justice.
> *Valentinian:* Justice shall never hear ye, I am justice.
>
> (III, 1)

The story, of course, lends itself admirably to sensational treatment. Though the dramas of Beaumont and Fletcher do not emphasize the theme of rape to the extent that Coleridge believed, no one can deny that it powerfully attracted them. The story of Lucrece finds repeated mention in their plays. The extremities of chastity and lust, moralizing and pornography, inexorably appealed to them. In *Valentinian* the crude bawdry of the panders admirably sets off the virginal purity of Lucina; the exquisite songs, the enticing display of jewels and the perfumed air of the court contrast strikingly with the sordid and violent action.

The episode of the rape Fletcher dramatizes with characteristic theatrical brilliance. As Act II ends and Valentinian leaves the stage with Lucina he ambiguously remarks:

> I dare not do it here, rise fair *Lucina*,
> I did but try your temper, ye are honest,
> And with the commendations wait on that.
> I'le lead ye to your Lord and give you to him;
> Wipe your fair eyes: he that endeavours ill,
> May well delay, but never quench his hell.
>
> (II, 4)

Act III opens with the exclamation:

> 'Tis done, Licinius!

In the theatre, the line must have sounded like a thunderclap. It is a key to a favourite Fletcherian device. His varied effects have often been noted, but his varied *tempi* much less remarked. The slow, cumulative effect of tragedy, the intensifying of tragic inevitability are not for him. The debates he inserts are designed to mark time, to heighten suspense, to titillate audience curiosity. At such moments the play has little forward action. But once a decision has been taken—usually off-stage—the play bounds forward again. Tragedy stalks not in stately robes with the deliberative pace of the cothurnus. Her draperies are in disarray. When she strides forward it is with seven-league boots.

The interim between Acts II and III of *Valentinian* would furnish many other dramatists with sufficient material for tragedy. One can well imagine the slow unweaving of the tangled web of will and passion in the hands of Racine. But Fletcher refuses to concentrate on the inner conflicts of Valentinian. A decision is suddenly taken. A deed is done. The action precipitates a new crisis and once again the play comes to a temporary standstill. Maximus and Aecius virtually overlook the ravished Lucina as they debate the validity of revenge upon the emperor. They relish the dilemma as good rhetoricians would. Maximus even ingeniously rationalizes his wife's rape:

> She knows
> I love no bitten flesh, and out of that hope
> She might be from me, she contrived this knavery.
> (III, 1)

The abrupt news of Lucina's death shocks him into more sober reflections. He leaves the stage to resolve his dilemma. When he next appears he has undergone a transformation. He has decided to betray his friend Aecius, the apologist for divine right, and through his death bring about the death of the emperor. Once again the psychological *scène à faire* has been omitted. These interior conflicts Fletcher rarely attempts to dramatize. As one would suspect, he makes little use of the soliloquy. The clash between individuals, the clash between the individual and convention, rather than the clash within the individual, usually make up the substance of his dramatized debates. Rarely can Fletcher conceive of the tragedy of the individual caught in an infernal machine of his own making. He concentrates instead on the tragedy of circumstance.

The series of tragi-comedies beginning with *The Mad Lover* (1615–19) and concluding with *A Wife for a Month* (1624) finds him much more at his ease. *The Mad Lover* marks a return to the theme of ways of love which figures so prominently in *The Faithful Shepherdess* and *Cupid's Revenge*. Memnon, a rugged veteran of the wars, through his love for the Princess Calis undergoes a transformation from a rough military buffoon to a deeply earnest lover. The soldier's rejection of the rigours of battle in favour of the softer pleasures of love earlier proved a favourite subject of Fletcher's. Here he treats his theme with greater seriousness, contrasting Memnon's love to that of his two rivals—his brother, Polydore, and his fellow-soldier, Syphax. The scene is Paphos, and the reigning goddess Venus, but a generally cynical view of love suffuses the play. From the bawdy and conniving priestess of Venus to the blunt, wench-hunting soldiery, all betray a moral corruption that culminates in a symbolic masque of beasts that died for love. Memnon himself bears the mark of the beast, as Fletcher indicates through Chilax's mocking imitation of the love-sick soldier. But Memnon is also capable of recognizing a deeper form of love.

> Pure love,
> That, that the soul affects, and cannot purchase
> While she is loaden with our flesh, that Love, sir,
> Which is the price of honour, dwells not here.
>
> (II, 1)

Through his refusal to take advantage of his brother's generous offer of Calis' hand, and through his heroic selflessness:

> Young man,
> You cannot overreach me in your goodness
>
> (V, 1)

he points forward to a long line of heroic lovers. At the same time he looks backward to the Platonic lovers of *The Faithful Shepherdess*. Grotesque as he often is, in contemplating, for example, the literal gift of his heart to his mistress, he stands out, nonetheless, as the most admirable figure in this tragi-comedy of the inadequacies of love.

The Loyal Subject (1618) as well, has a certain thematic unity—the duty of an individual to himself and to his sovereign. Adapted from an episode in Bandello, this story of the friction between a king and his counsellors underlies also Heywood's *The Royal King, The Loyal Subject* (c. 1602). Heywood's play analyses the relation of a sovereign to an over-generous subject, but Fletcher's play conspicuously alters Bandello to make Archas, the loyal subject, a prototype of honour. The play opens in the familiar court setting. A weak Duke has fallen prey to a swarm of flatterers and parasites.

> So many newborn Flies his light gave life to,
> Buzze in his beams, Flesh-flies, and Butterflies,
> Hornets, and humming Scarabs, that not one honey-Bee
> That's loaden with true labour, and brings home
> Encrease and Credit, can 'scape rifling,
> And what she sucks for sweet, they turn to bitterness.
>
> (II, 4)

The action nominally occurs in Moscow, and though Fletcher might have drawn upon his uncle Giles for authentic background material, he made no apparent effort to do so. Once again his locale seems closer to the precincts of Whitehall. The relationship between Archas, Boroskie, and the Duke also suggests certain English parallels, and a series of curious allusions in the play increase the temptation to read this as a political allegory.

Without question *The Loyal Subject* contains some explicit political comment, and certain details lead one to suspect that in creating Archas Fletcher once more had Raleigh in mind. Act III scene 5 makes little sense read otherwise. A mysterious Ancient, with the function of a chorus, cries out for brooms. A second soldier cries potatoes—a commodity associated with Raleigh. Elsewhere in the play we come across mention of Virginia. The Duke's seizure of Archas' treasure may also have called to mind James's seizure of Raleigh's estate at Sherborne. Archas, like so many others of the antique soldiers in Fletcher's plays, chafes against a stagnant peace, as Raleigh pleaded for more vigorous anti-Spanish policy. The identification must not be pressed too far, of course. (Fletcher puts into Archas' mouth, perhaps for reasons of discretion, an impassioned defence of kingship.) In themselves the individual details carry little weight, but put together they add up to fairly persuasive evidence.

In technique the play anticipates some of the later collaborations in tragi-comedy, both in its highly wrought situations and unexpected convolutions, and, like them, as Waith has observed, it relates to the *Controversiae* in extravagance of rhetoric and peculiarity of situation.

Fletcher's next unaided tragi-comedy, *The Humorous Lieutenant* (1619) has had probably more unanimous praise than any other play of this group. Hardly any of its elements, however, bear the stamp of originality. *The Mad Lover* and *The Nice Valour* both deal with a similar situation—the consuming passion of a hardened soldier (Demetrius) for an attractive coquette (Celia). Coupled with this, a 'humorous lieutenant' suffers, on a more physical plane, the pangs of an indiscreet attachment. On both these levels Fletcher finds himself thoroughly at home. He can treat in a farcical manner the caprices of the lieutenant, spurred by his malady into prodigies of valour on the battlefield, but reduced to lamblike meekness when he thinks himself cured. The clinical nature of this humour hardly deterred him. Nor, indeed, did such humour conspicuously violate seventeenth century comic decorum, with its penchant for venereal jesting. The homosexual foolery of the scenes in which the lieutenant mistakenly swallows a love philtre intended by the King Antigonus for Celia, also gave Fletcher no pause. 'There are few more laughable scenes in farcical literature than those in which the Lieutenant imagines himself to be a handsome wench of fifteen, woos the king most fatuously, even kisses the royal horses as they go by,'[6] Gayley comments, though he inexplicably feels a distaste for parallel scenes in other plays of Fletcher's.

On the more serious level of the main plot Fletcher also moves with assurance. Demetrius, general of the armies, falls deeply in love with Celia, but finds himself a rival to his father, Antigonus, and his arch-enemy, Seleucus. Like Memnon (*The Mad Lover*) Demetrius anticipates the lovers of heroic drama in his dedication to the transcendental ideals of love. But it is on Celia that Fletcher concentrates his attention. In her he achieves a successful fusion of the scornful lady and the romantic heroine. Although in love with Demetrius, she feels an irresistible compulsion to amuse herself at his expense. She takes an equal delight in countering and over-reaching the schemes of Antigonus and the bawd, Leucippe. Yet so recklessly does she play with the emotions of the serious-minded general that she provokes him into denouncing all womankind. Momentarily the action takes a serious turn. But the play cannot have other than a happy ending. Celia, like her

Restoration granddaughters, Angelica and Millamant, once she has asserted her independence, realizes that she values true devotion still more, and it is her witty resource and reluctant submission to love that chiefly account for the popularity of this play after 1660.

Few have ever cared, or are likely to care, for *Women Pleased* (1619–22). Like *The Two Noble Kinsmen* it derives from Chaucer, and the Wife of Bath's riddle ('What do women most desire?' 'Their will') serves as the basis for a two-tiered tragi-comedy that on neither level has the wit or energy of its source. The main plot tells the story of Silvio who, for his indiscreet wooing of the Princess Belvidere, is banished from the court for one year, at the end of which time he must answer a riddle or forfeit his life. During his exile Belvidere, disguised as a hag, comes to him and offers to help him fulfil the condition, provided that he will grant her one wish. At the appointed time she reappears, still disguised, saves his life by disclosing the solution to the riddle, and then expresses her one wish—marriage to Silvio. She mitigates the shock, however, by offering him a curious choice—will he have as his bride one fair, young, and fickle, or one old, ugly, and constant? Abashedly he replies, 'Into thy sovereign will I put my answer'. The ascendancy of her will once recognized, Belvidere unmasks and claims Silvio as her husband.

The subplot uses this same theme. Disguised as a merchant, Claudio, unsuccessful suitor to Belvidere, deserts the court and sets out to woo Isabella, the young wife of Lopez, 'a sordid usurer'. For four acts Fletcher spins out their amorous intrigue. In the last act, however, the playwright feels compelled to give this Italianate cuckolding story an abrupt twist and align it to the main plot. A sudden burst of generosity on Lopez' part induces him to offer Isabella what she has long wished for—financial independence. The effect upon her is as electrifying as Sir Peter's gratuitous generosity to Lady Teazle in *The School For Scandal.* During her final tryst with Claudio she unexpectedly turns upon him and bitterly upbraids him for trying to seduce her. He, no less surprisingly, reveals himself as her brother who, in the guise of a suitor, has secretly been testing her chastity.

The dramas of the first decades of the seventeenth century contain many examples of such chastity tests. But whether these tests involving the proving of mother, wife, or sister, the playwrights pointedly make us aware of the trial. Fletcher, in failing to do so, robs his situation of impact. Consequently Claudio's scenes with Isabella (can he have had *Measure For Measure* in mind?) have none of the moral suspense that characterizes, for example, Vindice's trial of Gratiana and Castiza in *The Revenger's Tragedy*. Both main and subplot of *Women Pleased* Fletcher concludes with a trick. Belvidere drops her mask of age. Isabella reasserts her virtue. In both plots the ugly duckling turns into a swan.

Fletcher's next play in this group, *The Island Princess* (1619–22), has considerably more merit. Possessing many of the standard features of tragi-comedy, its chief interest lies, however, in its deviations from this pattern. The opening scenes have a conventional enough air. Quisara, sister to the emprisoned king of Sidore, offers her hand to whomever of her suitors rescues her brother from captivity. Armusia, a Portuguese captain, succeeds in doing so, but his success enrages his rivals, and when the king returns he hears rumours that the Portuguese plan the spiritual and physical conquest of the island. A political crisis develops which suddenly brings about a head-on collision between the religions of the East and the West. Quisara, the island princess, finds herself torn between the Christianity of her husband, Armusia, and her ancestral Mohammedan faith.

It cannot be said, however, that a religious theme underlies this play. Fletcher uses religion merely as a catalyst to precipitate the intrigue. Quisara longs for the crown and the torments of martyrdom as does Dorothea in the nearly contemporary Massinger-Dekker *Virgin Martyr* (1620). But the two heroines have little in common. Massinger's play, spiced as it is with sex and spectacle, strikes an occasionally genuine religious note. Nothing in Fletcher's play can match the intensity of Dorothea's speeches as she ascends the scaffold (IV, 3). Quisara is posturing and attitudinizing like one of Bernini's saints. Her remarks as she observes Armusia's rugged constancy are enlightening:

> Your Faith, and your Religion must be like ye . . .
> I do embrace your faith, Sir, and your fortune;

Go on, I will assist ye, I feel a sparkle here,
A lively sparkle that kindles my affection,
And tells me it will rise to flames of glory.

(V, I)

She is already basking in a baroque 'gloire'. Corneille's Polyeucte also seeks his 'gloire' in martyrdom, but he elects his martyrdom through reason and not through passion. Quisara's motivation is entirely a transient emotional one.

The meretricious manner in which Fletcher flirts with his potentially serious theme finds unconsciously comic expression in the king's words in the final scene, after the opportune rescue of Quisara and Armusia by the Portuguese soldiery.

Take her friend—
You have half persuaded me to be a Christian.

(V, I)

The generally bemused and inept king states the case fairly. Fletcher's play can make no claim, however slight, as an early *pièce à thèse*. It is quite in keeping that the last scene discloses the religious controversy as a political manoeuvre instigated by the king of Sidore's arch-enemy. Fletcher has no real interest in the friction between East and West. He uses the Indian locale merely for its novelty, and in using this setting he has considerable success. One wishes, indeed, that he had indulged his taste for the oriental even further. Few passages in his work can match Armusia's lyric exaltation as he steps on the island shores:

We are arrived among the blessed Islands,
Where every wind that rises blows perfumes,
And every breath of air is like an Incence:
The treasure of the Sun dwells here, each Tree
As if it envied the old *Paradice*,
Strives to bring forth immortal fruit.

(I, I)

One can see why the later Restoration audiences, captivated by the exoticism of *The Indian Queen* and *The Indian Emperor*, welcomed Fletcher's play and delighted in the opportunities it provided for spectacular display.

Fletcher's last unaided tragi-comedy, *A Wife for a Month* (1624) reverts to the theme of a woman's honour. Sorano, a villainous parasite, repeatedly attempts to prostitute his sister, Evanthe, to the lecherous tyrant, Frederick. Her impregnable virtue frustrates and angers them, but the happy find of some verses addressed to her by her admirer, Valerio, suggests to them a consummate revenge.

> To be your own, but one poor Month, I'd give
> My Youth, my Fortune, and then leave to live.
>
> (I, 1)

Given this *donnée*, the play at once moves into high gear. Frederick orders Valerio to marry Evanthe for one month before being put to death, a highly literal and typically Fletcherian punishment. Evanthe, on her part, is sentenced to remarry within twelve months, under the same conditions, on pain of death. Despite the circumstances, Valerio joyfully accepts. The ensuing scenes Fletcher devotes to heightening the tension and sexual anticipation. He does so through careful characterization, particularly of Evanthe. In Act I she defends her honour with a militant display of virginity that betrays the intensely sensuous side of her nature: 'I would first take to me, for my lust, a Moor. One of your galley slaves . . . than be your Queen,' 'I hadst rather thou hadst me delivered to the pirates . . . and sold me to wild bawds'. Her keen physical expectations of her wedding-night come as no surprise.

The sensual Valerio is as skilfully drawn. But even before his wedding-night his anticipations are dashed. Sorano shows him the king's ring, forbids consummation of the marriage, and orders him to reveal nothing to Evanthe on pain of her death. Reluctantly he enters his bridal-chamber where the scene that follows recalls *The Maid's Tragedy* (II, 1). Amintor's shock parallels that of Evanthe as Valerio, obedient to the king's wishes, unexpectedly argues first for Platonic love and then pleads impotency. In *The Maid's Tragedy* Beaumont and Fletcher achieve much of their impact in the Amintor–Evadne scene through surprise and through skilful misdirection in the previous scenes. In *A Wife for a Month* Fletcher achieves a less sensational, but more legitimate scene, through careful preparation.

Throughout the play he maintains a high pitch of suspense through a series of artfully devised situations. Act IV, for example, containes two parallel temptation scenes. Frederick, the tyrant, taunts Valerio and offers him his life on condition that he resign Evanthe. Only after seeming to waver and capitulate does Valerio reassert himself and angrily refuse. Similarly, the bawdy Cassandra, like a devil's advocate, uses her subtlest pleas to tempt Evanthe:

> Had *Lucrece* e'r been thought of but for *Tarquin?*
> She was before a simple unknown woman,
> When she was ravish'd, she was reverend Saint;
> And do you think she yielded not a little?
> And had a kind of will to be re-ravished?
> Believe it, yes.

A catalogue of Frederick's Herculean powers compounds the temptation. Apparently on the verge of capitulation, Evanthe suddenly recovers her moral balance and angrily dismisses the bawd. But in no sense do these scenes dramatize a real inner conflict. The playwright aims at the exploitation of thrills, not at the probing of a moral crisis.

The usual twists and reversals characterize the progress of the action. Evanthe, stung by the rumour that Valerio has pleaded impotency to prolong his life, angrily confronts him with this charge. In answer to his explanation that he did so in order to save *her* life and not his own, she remarks simply: 'And was not I worthy to die nobly?' As a complete reconciliation between the two lovers seems imminent, an emissary of the king parts them with the reminder that their month of marriage has come to an end. The disappearance and reported death of Valerio compel Evanthe to choose another husband from a group of suitors, but these, once informed of the conditions of marriage to her, understandably lose interest in the match. So complicated is the climax that not even the reappearance of Valerio, disguised as a suitor, can resolve it. Instead, Fletcher invokes a *deus ex machina*—Alphonso, brother to Frederick. Miraculously cured of a melancholy adust (a poison has had the effect of a restorative), he leads a successful revolt against his tyrannical brother and brings about a happy union between Evanthe and Valerio.

Unexpected turnabouts of this sort abound in the play. Characters shift with chameleon facility. Few plays, indeed, illustrate more perfectly the ambivalent nature of tragi-comedy: 'it wants deaths, which is enough to make it no tragedy, yet brings some near it'. Fletcher's play calls to mind once more his lasting debt to Marston, particularly *The Malcontent*. The parallels go beyond merely superficial resemblances—corrupt Italian courts, rival dukes, feigned deaths, disguises, and peripeteia. Their fundamentally sceptical outlook, their emphasis on theatrical values, their tendency to wed morality and pornography—these have a far more deep-seated importance. Above all else, Fletcher enjoys his role as an illusionist. He conjures, he manipulates, he appears now in one guise, now in another, and on the stage of tragi-comedy he can assume this identity most effectively.

His unassisted comedies, as well, effectively demonstrate the play of these same talents. *The Woman's Prize, or The Tamer Tamed* has been variously dated from 1604–1617, though Baldwin Maxwell cogently argues for a date between 1610–1611.[7] As the title suggests, it bears some resemblance to *The Taming of the Shrew*, as does Fletcher's later comedy, *Rule a Wife and Have a Wife*. *The Woman's Prize* salvages from Shakespeare the names of Petruchio, Bianca, and Tranio, but they have little connection with their original namesakes. One can hardly read Fletcher's work, as McKeithan has attempted to do, as a continuation of Shakespeare's play. Katherine is dead. The Petruchio of Shakespeare's play has suffered psychic emasculation.

Like *The Sea Voyage* (1622–Fletcher-Massinger), *The Woman's Prize* unhappily anticipates 'Shakespeare improved'. In both plays Fletcher completely inverts and retailors his material. Prospero, the genius of the isle, is transformed into Rosellia, an enchantress. Petruchio is displaced by Maria, his second wife, as the tamer. Though not far removed in time from their Shakespearian sources, Fletcher's versions relate more closely to Davenant's Shakespearian adaptations. Shakespeare's poetry has disappeared from *The Sea Voyage* as completely as it has from the Dryden-Davenant *Tempest*. Shakespeare's plot and characters have been as tidily rearranged and balanced in *The Woman's Prize* as they are in the Davenant version of *Macbeth*.

In Fletcher's revision of *The Taming of The Shrew* Katherine is dead. The play begins as Petruchio marries for the second time. However, on his wedding-night the hot-blooded and boastful bridegroom finds himself locked out of his house by his wife, Maria. (Characteristically of Fletcher, wedding-nights occasion frustration far more often than consummation.) The taming of the tamer then begins. To counterbalance this main plot Fletcher devotes his subplot to Livia's wooing of the ineffectual Rowland. As in *The Wild Goose Chase* the males are clearly destined to go down to defeat. Petruchio proves no match for Maria. Driven to desperation, he finally feigns death and arranges to be carried in his coffin before her. Her unlooked-for exclamations over the wickedness and waste of his life so enrage him that he leaps up to protest and thereby suffers his final humiliation. But by then both Maria and Livia have wearied of indulging their wit at male expense and decide to take pity on the thoroughly chastened Petruchio and Rowland.

The epilogue of the play states as its theme, 'To teach both sexes due equality'. Taken out of context this gives the misleading impression that Fletcher intended this play as a tract. Only in the most farcical sense can this be said to be true. The city and country wives who come swarming to the rescue of the embattled Maria and Livia and, from the walls above defy mankind, bear some resemblance to the termagents of *Lysistrata*, but at no point does Fletcher make a serious plea for sexual equality. When Maria locks the door in Petruchio's face the slamming is not heard around the world as it is when Ibsen's Nora does so. Fletcher is merely exploiting a favourite theme—the battle of sexes—as he does also in *Rule a Wife and Have a Wife*, *Women Please*, and *The Spanish Curate*. The tone of *The Woman's Prize* never varies from that of high-spirited farce.

Monsieur Thomas (c. 1615), so Richard Brome noted, failed in its original production, though subsequent audiences appreciated its lively action, and it has won general critical approval. The plot centres on the comic dilemma which confronts Monsieur Thomas on his returns from his travels. His father, an antiquated roué of standard Fletcherian design, longs to see his son in the role of a witty, high-flying rake. Thomas's bride-to-be, Mary, on the other hand, pictures him in the role of a modest, domesticated lover. Through a series of unfortunate circumstances he succeeds in conveying to each one exactly the opposite impression. To his father he appears a clod; to his fiancée, a libertine. His father threatens him with disinheritance; his fiancée, with dismissal. His dilemma, which roughly anticipates that of Goldsmith's and Sheridan's comic heroes, has its happy resolution through a series of often coarsely farcical episodes.

The romantic subplot, drawn from the second part of d'Urfe's *L'Astrée,* strikes an altogether different note. It dramatizes the rivalry between the elderly Valentine and young Frank for the hand of Cellide. At many points these wooing plots, comic and serious, parallel each other. Frank's illness, for example, coincides with Thomas's feigned sickness. At other points Fletcher deliberately contrasts them strongly. In Act III we find juxtaposed a burlesque episode in which Thomas is enticed into bed with a blackamoor and a genuinely poignant scene between Cellide, Frank and Valentine. The subplot leads the play almost into the realms of tragi-comedy, but Fletcher refuses to violate the over-all comic tone and resolves the romantic deadlock with the usual trickery. The revelation that Valentine is really Frank's father causes the older man to concede Cellide to him. Thus Fletcher avoids the tragic implications in this triangle, and however much he wrenches probability to bring about this happy ending, in this play he does successfully blend farce and romantic comedy.

During the spring of 1621, in all probability, Fletcher completed *The Pilgrim* for the King's Company. As with many others of his works, this play has a Spanish source. But Fletcher's use of Lope de Vega's *El Peregrino en su Patria* (1604, translated into English 1621) clarifies neither the nature or the extent of his knowledge of Spanish literature.[8] Fitz-Maurice Kelly refused to believe that he could read Spanish at all.[9] E. M. Wilson, in tracing *Rule a Wife and Have a Wife* to an untranslated Spanish novel, has denied this and demonstrated that Fletcher's play makes use of phrases literally translated from the original.[10] In other instances (e.g. *The Custom of the Country*) Fletcher apparently used English translations of Spanish novels. With typical Elizabethan inconsistency he appears to have worked sometimes from the Spanish and sometimes from English translations. The dubious argument that Fletcher possibly saw various Spanish works in manuscript translations has little validity, and few now doubt that he had some command of Spanish.

It would be pleasant to ascribe to him also some knowledge of the contemporary Spanish stage. He would have appreciated Lope de Vega's torrential outpourings and the business-like attitude toward the theatre he expressed in the *Arte Nuevo:* 'Since the crowd pays for the comedies, it is fitting to talk foolishly to it to satisfy its tastes'. One can imagine Ben Jonson's vigorous disapproval of this obsequious deference to the vulgar. One can imagine, as well, Fletcher's approbation. Like Lope he doubtless kept Plautus and Terence in his study but put them aside when the time came to write a comedy. Like Lope he made his obeisance to Aristotle and Horace, but at the same time he winked broadly at the pit.

The typical pattern of Lope de Vega, the *comedia di capa y espada*, has unquestioned similarities to the Beaumont and Fletcher conception of tragi-comedy. Establishing a direct link between them, however, has proved a treacherous undertaking. Schelling's discussion of *Foreign Influences on the Elizabethan Drama* points out as many disparities as similarities between the two types, and the astonishing parallels between the physical stages of Spain and England made certain likenesses almost inevitable.[11]

Comparative studies of the Elizabethan drama and the drama of Spain's golden age abound with perils and temptations. From the time of Marlowe to Shirley we come across the same stimulating and exasperating analogues. But the relationship, if any, between Marlowe's *Tamburlaine* and Lope de Vega's dramatization of his career is no easier to establish than that between Shirley's *The Young Admiral* and its Spanish original. Fletcher's use of Spanish sources makes the relationship no clearer. He can have no scruples as to looting the Spanish drama. The Elizabethans took a tolerant view of piracy in general—particularly from the Spanish. Yet the only works appropriated by Fletcher were Spanish novels. Did he feel disdain for the Spanish drama? Did he have no access to it? Were the *sueltas* that circulated through Europe unavailable in England? Such problems may yet be elucidated on a more general scale, but probably not through a study of Fletcher. Certainly *The Pilgrim* casts no light upon them, but it is worth reading as one of Fletcher's happiest experiments in the comedy of Hispanic intrigue.

Of all his later comedies, however, *The Wild Goose Chase* (c. 1621) gave Fletcher the greatest satisfaction. We know that its author joined happily in the applause on the occasion of its first production by The King's Men. Successfully revived before the Commonwealth, it also enjoyed publication as a separate Folio in 1652, and a subsequent long life on the Restoration stage.

Few Stuart plays capture as well the gaiety and ebullience of the period. Though the scene nominally transpires in Paris, the playwright soon forgets this, and his play so realistically mirrors Jacobean London that even during the reign of James I's grandsons, the milieu was still instantly recognizable.

Superficially this play seems no more than a random patchwork of intrigues often used earlier by Fletcher. But it strikingly demonstrates how Fletcher's mastery of tragi-comedy could be turned to effective use for comic purposes. Henry Haringdon's prefatory verses to the 1652 Folio pay deserved tribute to the masterly ordering of the plot, and few Elizabethan or Jacobean plays can be as neatly disassembled.

In Act I Fletcher introduces his main characters—Mirabell, Pinac and Belleur, three attractive young rakes, and Oriana, Rosalura and Lilia-Bianca, three appealing young women. With Act II the intrigue develops rapidly. Mirabell vaingloriously boasts of Oriana's consuming desire for him, and Pinac and Belleur confidently begin their wooing of Rosalura and Lilia-Biance. All three are clearly destined to be punished by the ladies. Their discomfiture soon begins. Lilia-Bianca, a 'starcht piece of austerity' in Act I, astonishes Pinac by her effrontery in Act II; the lascivious Rosalura of the opening scene coldly rebukes Belleur's impassioned courtship, Through these comic turnabouts the ladies set out to humble their arrogant suitors.

The machinations to subjugate Mirabell begin in Act III. By then Pinac and Belleur have already suffered humiliation, but the ladies' main victim remains unscathed. The stratagems to punish him get under way when De Gard, Oriana's brother, comes disguised as a suitor to her, attempts to arouse Mirabell's jealousy, and forces a quarrel with him. Mirabell, however, sees through the trick and laughingly exposes De Gard. Act IV repeats this same plot pattern. In the first two scenes Lilia-Bianca and Rosalura pretend repentance for their imposture, but only to humiliate and overreach Pinac and Belleur once again. The remainder of the act is devoted to a second stratagem to entrap Mirabell. On this occasion Oriana feigns lunacy to attract his sympathetic attention. But once again he sees through the plot. Gravely he announces that he would marry her if she were only sane again. Too quickly Oriana recovers—to Mirabell's mocking laughter. But the final act brings about the triumph of Oriana. Lilia-Bianca and Rosalura have by that time sufficiently humbled Pinac and Belleur and have generously accepted them as suitors. Inspired by their success, Oriana undertakes the final conquest of Mirabell and, disguised as an Italian lady, she entraps the by-now resigned Mirabell into marriage. Quite obviously he has no more chance of escape than does John Tanner from Ann Whitefield in Shaw's *Man and Superman*.

Surprise, comic peripeteia, misleading characterization—all these devices of tragi-comedy contribute to the speed and amusement of the play. And as tragi-comedy relies on a series of shocks and catastrophes, a pulsating series of climaxes, so this comedy has its basis in a series of intrigues. But there is no basic comic situation or attitude which prevails, as there is no individual tragic situation or view of life which dominates Fletcher's tragedies. Though the reduction of the three males is accomplished with almost mathematical precision, the ordering of the comic skirmishes is, ultimately, of little importance. The tricks may be played in almost any order. The strategic victory must fall to the ladies—that is all. In this amorous warfare the play looks backward to *Love's Labour's Lost* and *Much Ado About Nothing*, but it anticipates as well the witty contretemps of the beaux and belles of Restoration comedy.

For his next comedy Fletcher drew once again upon the Spanish source of greatest inspiration to him—Cervantes. No less than seventeen plays of the Beaumont and Fletcher canon, Schelling argues, show traces, or deeper influences, of the Spanish master. *Rule a Wife and Have a Wife* (acted 1624) derives from *El Casamiento Engañoso*, one of the *Exemplary Novels*, and *El Sagaz Estacio*, but the original source of the subplot, an ironic tale of the biter bit, Fletcher transforms into broad comedy by altering and lightening the entire spirit of the original story and by injecting a variety of humours.

For the main plot he reverts to a theme often used by him before—the sexual clash in marriage. As in his earlier play, *The Woman's Prize* (1604-17), he draws upon *The Taming of The Shrew* for inspiration. Yet neither play of Fletcher's relates too closely to Shakespeare's comedy. Undoubtedly some features of *Rule a Wife*—the theme, the shrewish wife and the unexpectedly resourceful tamer—derive from Shakespeare, but the essential business Fletcher fills in himself, and it is his high-spirited management of the plot that sweeps the play along irresistibly.

From start to finish it is a play for actors. Action abounds, and the clearly drawn characters, like those of Farquarh, midway between realistic comedy and the comedy of humours, stand out in bold relief. One wonders to what extent Fletcher wrote with his eye on individual actors. Lists of *dramatis personae* often give us a clue, but these sometimes refer not to the original production but to subsequent revivals. Of the Jacobean actors in the King's Company we know distressingly little. We can speak with some assurance of the impact which Betterton, Mrs. Barry and Mrs. Bracegirdle had on the drama between 1680 and 1700, but it is difficult to make such speculations about Jacobean actors. Nevertheless, in such a work as Baldwin Maxwell's studies in Beaumont and Fletcher we can gain insight into Fletcher's sensitive awareness of the capacities of individual actors.

The part of Leon in *Rule a Wife* offers a case in point. Professor Maxwell suggests that in creating Leon, Fletcher had John Lowin in mind.[12] Very probably this is so. Fletcher's careful attribution of physical qualities to some of his characters would indicate the justice of such a supposition. Yet, if it is a part for a specific actor, it is also a part for *an* actor. Fletcher's awareness of movement and sense of the stage make an obvious appeal to any actor. Take, for example, the opening dialogue in the scene of young Leon's first meeting with Margarita.

Margarita: Can you love a young Lady? How he blushes!
Altea: Leave twirling of your hat and hold your head up
And speak to th' lady.
(II, 1)

It is no wonder that generations of actors have delighted in this play and have found in such roles as the Copper Captain (Michael Perez), Estifania and Cacafogo admirable opportunities to display their talents.

Not only in the action but in speech as well, the author shows his consideration for the actors. The language, despite its often gross directness and coarseness, has the pulse of life and the poetry of life. The lines break and shift in tempo. One senses the drive behind them, and one senses how closely the dialogue of this play, despite its Spanish setting, resembles a transcript of cracking Jacobean conversation. But Fletcher is capable of lyric expression as well. Though the failure of *The Faithful Shepherdess* discouraged him from attempting to achieve a sustained lyricism in his later plays, he retains to the end of his career, like Ben Jonson, a capacity to vary his effects from the most silvery blank verse to the most robust, life-like prose.

No less than *The Wild Goose Chase*, *Rule a Wife* has a deliberate, if not immediately apparent, architecture. To counterbalance the main plot, the taming of Margarita by Leon, Fletcher adds a sub-plot, the taming of Perez by Estifania. He makes use also of careful parallelism in his comic peripeteia. Thus in III, 4, the fortune-hunting Perez finds he has been caught in his own noose by the wily Estifania who has passed herself off as the mistress of a large household. In the very next scene the bashful Leon astounds his wife and the guests at his wedding-banquet by unexpectedly revealing a will of iron. The discrepancy between appearance and reality, the occasion of so many situations in tragi-comedy, Fletcher here uses to fine comic effect.

The morality of the comedy leaves something to be desired, perhaps. The Duke's pontifical summation:

> And all the world shall know, a noble mind
> Makes women beautiful, and envie blind.
>
> (V, 1)

suggests that at the close Margarita has achieved this state of grace. But before the pleasure-hungry Margarita can be chastened and beautified, Leon is forced to resort to somewhat violent and unorthodox means that culminate when he accuses her of intrigue, bullies her physically, and threatens her with the humiliation of watching him lie with her maid. This final shock therapy has its intended effect. She kneels to him, exclaiming:

> I have lost, my self Sir,
> And all that was my base self, disobedience.
>
> (V, 1)

Tender-minded critics might well question the morality of such a cure. But we must not forget the overwhelmingly male nature of the Jacobean drama. (It was a hundred years before *A Woman Killed With Kindness* was displaced by *The Careless Husband*.) Yet even in a period that paid little attention to moral quibbles, one must admit that Fletcher seems notably casual. Occasionally he can rise to noble eloquence, as in Leon's peroration on the duties of a husband (III, 5), but he feels few moral convictions deeply. More often than not, as Gayley points out, he avoids the moral issue by walking around it. At other times, in this play, for example, he seems simply unaware of it. *Rule a Wife and Have a Wife* makes no pretence to arrive at a morality of marriage. Fletcher remains content merely to amuse his audience with a brisk and entertaining comedy of intrigue.

Of *The Chances* (1613–1625) little need be said. This story of two highly-mettled young benedicts' adventures with a foundling also has its origin in Cervantes' *Exemplary Novels*, though the playwright, as usual, substitutes a farcical ending for a sentimental one. Its long life on the stage, first in Buckingham's Restoration version, then in Garrick's well-scrubbed eighteenth century version, may be attributed to its energetic intrigue, the vigour of the dialogue, and the life-like characterizations of Don John, Don Frederick, their landlady Gillian, and the impressible Antonio.

The prologue, written for a revival shortly before the Commonwealth, invites us to read this as a semi-biographical account of the playwright's early years.

> Ingenious Fletcher made it, he
> Being in himself a perfect comedie,
> And some sit here, I doubt not, dare aver
> Living he made that house a theatre
> Which he pleased to frequent.

Certainly the *ménage* of Don John and Don Frederick calls to mind Aubrey's account of Beaumont and Fletcher's Southwark lodgings:

> They lived together on the Banke side, not far from the Playhouse, both batchelors; lay together; had one Wench in the house between them, which they did so admire; the same cloathes and cloak, &c.; between them.[13]

However slight this biographical element may actually be, the play contains a passage which well expresses Fletcher's self-estimate as a comic writer. In the final scene Vecchio, the illusionist, makes an *apologia* that sums up this play and Fletcher's own comic attitude:

> My end is mirth,
> And pleasing, if I can, all parties.

NOTES TO CHAPTER THREE

1. Coleridge ms. note on *Valentinian* in Lamb's 1679 Folio, p. 384, now in the British Museum.

2. Baldwin Maxwell, *Studies in Beaumont, Fletcher and Massinger,* Chapel Hill, University of North Carolina, 1939, p. 78.
3. Charles Gayley, *Beaumont the Dramatist,* New York, 1914, p. 278.
4. Lawrence B. Wallis, *Fletcher, Beaumont and Company,* New York, 1947, pp. 210–216.
5. Fredson T. Bowers, *Elizabethan Revenge Tragedy,* Princeton University Press, 1940, pp. 184–216.
6. Gayley, *Beaumont the Dramatist,* p. 402.
7. Maxwell, *Studies,* pp. 29–45.
8. E. M. Wilson, 'Did John Fletcher read Spanish?' *Philological Quarterly,* XXVII (1948), pp. 187–190; Richard A. Impola, *Fletcher's Spanish Sources,* unpublished Columbia M. A. thesis, 1950.
9. J. Fitzmaurice Kelly, *Relations between Spanish and English Literature,* Liverpool University Press, 1910, p. 22.
10. E. M. Wilson, '*Rule A Wife and Have A Wife* and *El Sagaz Estacio*', *Review of English Studies,* XXIV (1948), pp. 189–194.
11. Felix E. Schelling, *Foreign Influences in Elizabethan Plays,* New York, 1923, p. 123.
12. Maxwell, *Studies,* p. 74n.
13. John Aubrey, *Brief Lives,* ed. Oliver Dick, London, 1950, p. 21.

FOUR

FLETCHER'S LATER COLLABORATIONS

THE record of John Fletcher's collaborations is a particularly confused one. He stands amid a group of figures some of whom are readily discernible—Beaumont, Massinger, Shakespeare. Others remain in the shadows—Field, Rowley, Daborne, Webster. The early Stuart playwrights had as notable a predilection for joint efforts as Hollywood scenario writers. The already complex problems of attribution become still more so when we consider that many of the plays underwent later revision. In Fletcher's case there is little point in discussing some of these works of dubious authorship and merit—sometimes both. We need pay little attention to *The Night Walker* (revised by Shirley in 1633), the highly conjectural *A Very Woman* (1634), or *The Maid in the Mill*, Fletcher's insignificant 1623 collaboration with William Rowley.

Only two of Fletcher's collaborators, beside Beaumont, deserve attention—Philip Massinger and William Shakespeare, and of the two the association with Massinger is by far the more important one.[1] In 1613 Beaumont married and retired to lead the life of a country gentleman. Three years later he died. Fletcher's mercurial temperament needed a steadying hand, and Beaumont had served as an effective check on his witty effervescence. Neither dramatist had worked best alone. Their combined genius exceeded the sum of their individual talents, and together they perfected a dramatic *genre* which Fletcher made use of for the rest of his life. But if he was unsuited to individual creative effort before 1613, he was still more so afterward. Clearly tragi-comedy had begun to bore him. As John Dryden later did, he found himself committed to reproducing his early dramatic successes. Fortunately, as a popular dramatist, Fletcher had little trouble finding a collaborator to alleviate this drudgery, and in Massinger he discovered a particularly useful assistant. He had something of the gravity and balance of Beaumont. He was industrious and, so far as we can judge, gratifyingly amenable to Fletcher's suggestions. Seventeenth century dramatic collaboration was, after all, scarcely 'collaboration' in our sense of the term. It was not based on the ideal of a conceptually unified dramatic work, but rather on the simple principle of a division of labour. Fletcher, in this case, dictated the terms, and he reserved for himself the spoils, much as the fashionable eighteenth century portrait painters concentrated on the hands and faces of their sitters but left the routine chores of portraiture to their assistants.

In some instances a dramatic project could be neatly divided into plot and subplot (*The Custom of the Country*, *The Spanish Curate*). In others the play could be roughly sketched out and divided up into acts. By far the greater proportion of plays in the Fletcher-Massinger canon fall into this second category. Fletcher's boredom with exposition and conclusion in most cases imposed the task of writing the first and final acts upon Massinger. As a reward, perhaps, Fletcher permitted his disciple the scenes of debate and the trial scenes (*The Spanish Curate*, *The Queen of Corinth*, *Sir John Barnavelt*). The non-literary nature of Elizabethan and Stuart drama accorded with this conception. The tendency to view the drama as a collection of individual scenes (the spectator's attitude) rather than as a unified tragic or comic action (the reader's attitude) encouraged this haphazard method. Of all the plays in the Elizabethan and Stuart canon, the plays of collaboration have perhaps suffered most at the hands of time. Our modern emphasis on conceptual unity, our studies in ideas, imagery, and psychology have led us to praise Webster and Ford, who had comparatively little praise in their own day, at the expense of Beaumont, Fletcher and Massinger, who had so much.

Fletcher and Massinger, for their tragi-comedies of collaboration, at least partially merit this neglect. They are turned out as mechanically as the well-made plays in the factories of Scribe and Sardou. *The Honest Man's Fortune* (1613), probably one of their earliest, may be chosen as typical. It is a synthetic product. The authors are no longer drawing on life but on literature. It is 'literary' in the worst sense of the word. In the earlier tragi-comedies Beaumont and Fletcher had created a dramatic tradition from the materials of Stuart court life. Here Fletcher and Massinger hold the mirror up to Art. 'I took example by two or three plays that methought concerned me,' exclaims Veramour in this play. Actually the playwrights are doing much the same thing. They synthesize; they rearrange materials kaleidoscopically. A slight alteration of the same constituent parts suffices to create still another play.

The Honest Man's Fortune tells the story of Montague, a much abused French lord, who falls from high to low estate, before rising once more to prosperity. For five acts he stoically endures the buffets of fortune, the machinations of a scheming trio, and and various humiliating trials of love before he finally proves himself. The theme of Fortune, the French setting, the testing of Montague, and his relationship to the Duchess of Orleans all suggest this play has an affinity to *Bussy D'Ambois*. Nathan Field who scored a great success as Chapman's hero, also appeared in *The Honest Man's Fortune*, almost certainly as Montague. But the Fletcher-Massinger tragi-comedy has little of the impact of Chapman's play. 'Fortune, not reason, rules the state of things,' observes Chapman bitterly as he studies the effect of a second-generation Tamburlaine's *virtu* upon the decadent French court. Fletcher's apostrophe to Fortune has a noble ring to it:

> Man is his own star, and that soul that can
> Be honest, is the only perfect man

but his male Cinderella story has little heroic quality. The moral tag, in this case, as in so many others, means very little. Montague possesses only a limited measure of integrity; his creators, still less. They play all the tricks they know. They dazzle and confuse the spectator with the well-tested devices of tragi-comedy. The latter scenes of Act I offer a fine instance of this sleight-of-hand. (Their dramatic reversals seem particularly Fletcherian, but perhaps Massinger had already learned the lesson of the master.)

The Duke of Orleans accuses his wife of being mistress to Montague. She denies this. Her brother, angered by the charge, threatens the Duke. The Duchess suddenly confesses her guilt, but after her brother leaves reveals to the Duke that she has made the admission only to stop bloodshed. When, later, her brother furiously confronts Montague, the Duchess bursts in to explain the lie. No sooner has her brother, calmed, taken his departure, than Montague, to the Duchess's horror, begins to make passionate love to her. Her indignation leads him in turn to disclose that he has merely been testing her chastity.

The dramatic use to which the authors put Veramour, Montague's page, is also characteristic. The breeches heroine, by this time, had become commonplace. From all appearances, Veramour belongs alongside Viola, Rosalind and Bellario. Veramour's passionate devotion to Montague, Veramour's agitation at the apparent signs of love between Montague and Charlotte, and Veramour's name all invite us to regard Veramour as a girl before the authors, in the final scene, reveal Veramour as a man.

The Queen of Corinth (c. 1617) and *The Knight of Malta* (c. 1618) have found general acceptance as the joint work of Fletcher, Massinger, and Nathan Field.[2] Of all the tragi-comedies these, perhaps, abound with the most sensations and surprises. They make use of traditional materials. Even Fletcher's language has an echo. Curious phrases recur—'Potch'd eggs with the souls suckt out'—or commonplaces—'Death hath a thousand doors'. Yet the plays make a virtue out of artifice.

To Field, as the junior collaborator, fell the dramatic chores. His capacity as an actor Fletcher was aware of through his performance in *The Coxcomb* and *The Honest Man's Fortune*. He had been on the stage since the age of thirteen, when he made his debut in *Cynthia's Revels*, and had joined the King's Men, Fletcher's company, in 1617. The Dulwich portrait of the young actor, with his intensely dark liquid eyes and quivering, sensuous mouth, suggests how effective Field must have been in the part of Miranda, the Knight. Though Fletcher reserved for himself the prize scene in *The Knight of Malta* in which Miranda, the probationary knight, attempts to violate Luscinda, a Turkish captive (III, 2), Field in the last act also provided fine opportunities for virtuoso acting when, before, the assembled Knights of Malta, the villain Mountferrat is stripped of his order and Miranda solemnly invested.

Field's contribution to the *Queen of Corinth* is generally believed to be Acts III and IV. The portrait of Onos, the young traveller, resembles that of Sir Abraham Ninny in his own play, *A Woman is a Weathercock* (1612), and his satire has the harshness and crudity that suggests the work of an enthusiastic but undisciplined son of Ben. The main interest in the *Queen of Corinth*, however, lies in Massinger's contribution (I and V). At the climactic point of the play the following situation has been developed: Theanor, the lustful, Cloten-like son of the Queen of Corinth, appears in court to answer two separate charges of rape brought by two different women. The penalty exacted may be either death or marriage. One woman demands his execution; the other demands marriage. As Eugene Waith has shown, this dilemma, based on one of the Senecan *controversiae*, furnishes the occasion for verbal fireworks and the full exercise of rhetorical prowess.[3] That the audience has suspended the laws of dramatic possibility must be assumed. 'Smaller things must give way to a striking scene,' to use Mr. Puff's words. The display of ingenuity in argument must justify the *donnée*. A *coup de théâtre*, the discovery that one woman has actually been raped twice, resolves the difficulty, but not before the possibilities of the impasse have been thoroughly explored. Similarly *The Laws of Candy* (c. 1619) draws upon the *controversiae* for a carefully developed trial scene. The laws of Candy ordain death as the punishment for ingratitude. Before the assembled Senate three individuals so charge each other. Finally the Senate itself is accused. The charges and countercharges lead to a scene of considerable complexity (almost Pirandelloesque in its study of the multiplicity of truth) before the invocation of a second law of Candy cuts through the legal tangle and resolves the situation.

The next tragi-comedy collaborated upon by Fletcher and Massinger, *The Custom of the Country* (c. 1620), represents one of their most sensational efforts. No play of theirs has had more general condemnation. On aesthetic grounds it can at least be partially defended. It is difficult, however, to deny Dryden's assertion that this play contains more bawdry than all the Restoration play put together. Swinburne's admiration for its audacity and magnificence is shrill and adolescent. Most critics have altogether disregarded it or cited it as a glaring example of the depths to which Fletcher was prepared to descend.

Its merit lies in the sheer technical dexterity with which three stories are woven together, though so close is the texture that readers merit the friendly caution in the prologue: ' 'Twill crave attention in the most, Because one point unmarked, the whole is lost'. In Cervantes' *Persiles Y Sigismunda* Fletcher and Massinger found highly suitable dramatic material. (The opening theme of *droit de seigneur* and Rutilio's adventures as a stallion in a male bawdy-house are Fletcher's calculatedly pornographic additions.) The episodes involving Duarte have a particular interest. The young braggart's passion for duelling leads to his near-death in a forced quarrel (a favourite theme of Fletcher's and paralleled closely in *A Very Woman*).[4] His antagonist, Rutilio, thinking he has killed the young man, flees and seeks refuge in a stranger's house. Its owner is Guiomar, mother of Duarte, who takes pity on Rutilio when he tells her that in defence of his honour he has killed an unknown adversary who has provoked a duel. No sooner has she concealed him than officers bring in the body of her son, given up for dead. Her wish to avenge her son and her obligation to protect the stranger under her roof lead to a moral crisis typical of the Spanish theatre, which Calderon makes use of in *Gil Perez*. (The would-be rape of Florimel in *The Maid in the Mill* invites further unfavourable comparison to Calderon's similar situation in *The Mayor of Zalamea*.) In *The Custom of the Country* Guiomar's moral dilemma attracts only passing attention. Her woes are soon forgotten. Even the favourite Fletcherian theme of duelling is given perfunctory treatment that in no way approaches the thoughtfulness of Middleton's approach in *A Fair Quarrel* (III, 1).

However dubious may be one's estimate of these tragi-comedies the sense of the stage and the mastery of pattern they display is notable. In the group of seven so-called 'historical' tragedies in which Fletcher and Massinger collaborated they seem far less assured. *Thierry and Theodoret* seems little more than a pastiche of elements from tragi-comedies; *Barnavelt* resembles chronicle history rather than tragedy; *Rollo, or The Bloody Brother,* moves almost exclusively on the plane of pathology;

The False One and *The Prophetess* conclude happily, and *The Lover's Progress* defies any of the more usual definitions of tragedy.

Massinger seems to have been of little use to Fletcher in developing a concept of tragedy. *Bonduca* and *Valentinian* had already indicated Fletcher's incapacity in this respect. Massinger's deeply felt opinions re-emphasized Fletcher's tendency to posture and declaim and Massinger's strong moral bias did not help either of them to appreciate the ambivalences and complexities of tragedy. This group of plays is, in fact, neither tragic nor historical. *The False One*, their version of the Caesar-Cleopatra story, is conceived of in terms that would have appealed to Tiepolo, whose Labia Palace frescoes of Cleopatra evoke much the same atmosphere. The display is sumptuous, the appeal highly theatrical, but it is postured and superficial.

Lamb's comment on *Thierry and Theodoret* (c. 1617) shows his insight into the essential emptiness of such tragedy when he writes of Fletcher: 'He seems to have thought nothing great could be produced in the ordinary way.'[5] The sense of straining after effect is in this play particularly marked. It moves with the pace and apparent purposelessness of a tornado. *Rollo* (c. 1619) suffers from much the same defects. Clearly based on *Richard III*, as Coleridge noted, its protagonist is a madman, his victims mere dummies. Even its sound and fury have a cracked ring to them. Sophia, Matilda, and Edith echo the three gloomy queens of Shakespeare's play, and Rollo's wooing of Edith unmistakably recalls Richard's wooing of Anne. Neither this play nor *Thierry and Theodoret* has a well-conceived tragic figure nor a consistently developed tragic situation. Nevertheless, both plays contain powerful individual scenes. Act IV, scene 1 of *Thierry and Theodoret*, in particular, Lamb hailed as the finest scene in Fletcher. Thierry has been told his lost virility will be restored to him if he slays the first woman he sees emerging from the temple of Diana at sunrise. At the appointed time he confronts a veiled woman who reveals herself as Ordella, his wife. Her constancy in the face of death shatters Thierry's resolution and he rushes off, unable to carry out the condition. The scene is indeed a notable one in its mood of Roman pathos and resignation. But the scene is a moral demonstration within a particular situation. It can be as readily detached from the framework of the play as the Stoic death scene which Addison later devised for Cato. It is a test of supreme tragedy such as Shakespeare's that individual scenes can be detached from context, yet lose much by being removed. Like the individual panels of an oriental screen, they belong to the overall design. Fletcher's and Massinger's scenes can be removed from context with almost no perceptible loss.

The False One also invites comparison to Shakespeare, though in this work the playwrights deal with an earlier period in Cleopatra's history—her rivalry with her brother Ptolemy and her conquest of Caesar. The title is a misleading one. The False One refers not to Cleopatra but to Septimius, a Roman double-dealer, whose part in the action marks the collaborators only real addition to their source material from Plutarch and Shakespeare. In all likelihood the playwrights intended him as a portrait of Sir Lewis Stukeley, whom James had used as his instrument in arresting and executing Sir Walter Raleigh.[6] The parallel has been convincingly argued, and Fletcher's apparent other allusions to Raleigh, his affectionate portraits of gruff old soldiers and Massinger's known political leanings tend to substantiate this ascription. His function resembles that of Alexas, the villainous eunuch in Dryden's *All For Love*. Both are used to siphon off the unpleasant aspects of Cleopatra's personality. In both Fletcher's and Dryden's play she is cast in the heroic mould. But the serpent of old Nile has lost her infinite variety. Cleanth Brooks' brilliant essay *On The Death Of Elizabethan Tragedy* points out the disastrous consequences of Dryden's 'scientific' use of tragedy to demonstrate a thesis or underline a moral.[7] If *All For Love* represents the *rigor mortis* of tragedy, in *The False One* its death throes have already begun. There is a chill dignity to Massinger's first and last acts, but neither the magnificence or Fletcher's masque of Nilus nor the rapidity of the action can conceal the play's essential hollowness, its dangerously oversimplified concept of character and situation.

The Prophetess (1622) has as little tragic urgency or complexity. In this spectacular entertainment Delphia, a powerful enchantress and white magician, as Prospero is, never permits the action to veer too close to the borders of tragedy. Of *The Double Marriage*

(c. 1620) and *The Lover's Progress* (1623) little need be said. Both are marked by alternate scenes of comedy and melodrama and contain isolated and splendid instances of formal rhetoric. Both fully utilize the resources of the Stuart stage. Their relationship to the tragi-comedies Eugene Waith has established in relating the basic dilemma of *The Double Marriage* to the *controversiae*, and indubitably the conclusion of this play, culminating in the deaths of Virolet and Juliana, relates to the world of tragi-comedy rather than tragedy.

The other play of this group, *Sir John Van Olden Barnavelt* (1619) comes at least closer to genuine historical tragedy than any of the others. Although based on a contemporary incident (the Dutch patriot Barnavelt was executed, in May, 1619) the play was not published until 1883. Clearly the authorities viewed it with suspicion as the long delay in publication and the excision of an allusion to Raleigh's execution make clear. With Middleton's *A Game at Chess* and Chapman's French tragedies, it stands almost alone in dealing with contemporary events. The career of Barnavelt offered Fletcher and Massinger great opportunities, but they failed to realize them. The Prince of Orange and Barnavelt excepted, the characters are pasteboard figures. Obviously the play was constructed with haste and had for English audiences the immediacy of a newsreel. To Massinger fell the task of dramatizing Barnavelt the politician; to Fletcher, Barnavelt the man. The speed with which they worked accounts at least in part for the play's prolix and careless structure. Scenes with grief-stricken children abound. Leidenberck's suicide is related no less than three times, and Barnavelt's constancy in the face of death is demonstrated interminably.

Problems of censorship also obviously hampered the collaborators. One senses throughout a disparity between what the authors felt and what they felt they could express. Both clearly disliked absolutism, and though Fletcher had more conservative views than those of Massinger, neither could afford to air his politics too freely. Perhaps for this reason the Prince of Orange during the first four acts appears as wise, sympathetic, tolerant and just, while Barnevelt, far less sympathetically drawn, is shown as a proud malcontent, concealing his pride and ambition under the cloak of religion. Only in the last act do the playwrights make a deliberate attempt to render him more appealing. Fletcher's grotesque second scene in Act V, in which the executioners play at dice for the honour of putting Barnavelt to death, has strongly suggestive overtones that invite us to view him as a misunderstood victim of persecution. But it is too late. The tragic vision is blurred. The play has no true centre.

Of all the Fletcher-Massinger collaborations, their comedies, much as they vary in quality, have perhaps the greatest interest. The earliest of these, *The Little French Lawyer* (c. 1619) has little to recommend it. For three acts it concentrates on the favourite Fletcherian anti-duelling theme, but the last two acts are hopelessly padded in Fletcher's best, or worst, scabrous style. *The Spanish Curate* (1622), drawn from an English translation of a Spanish novel, is scarcely better, though Fletcher's interpolation in III, 2, of an antiphonal dialogue between the Curate, Don Diego and the Puritan parishioners is justly celebrated.

Far more interest attaches to *The Sea Voyage* (1622). Clearly inspired by *The Tempest*, this play foreshadows the Dryden-Davenant adaptation of this romantic comedy. The plot is an even more wildly improbable one than Shakespeare's. A spectacular storm at sea shipwrecks a crew upon the shores of a female Commonwealth. Under the leadership of the Amazonian Rosellia, a group of scornful ladies seize upon the men for breeding purposes and, in typically Fletcherian fashion, agree to submit to them as wives for a month. Later, convinced that their husbands-to-be are pirates, the ladies turn upon their would-be consorts, bind them, and prepare to torture them to 'horrid music' when the providential appearance of Rosellia's long-lost husband, thought seized by the pirates, brings about a happy conclusion. Everywhere the play is marked by haste and carelessness. No less than four shipwrecks occur. Rosellia and her husband, Sebastian, though marooned on the same island, fail to meet until the last act. Crude parallels to Shakespeare's play abound. Prospero has changed his sex to become Rosellia; Lamure, Franville, and Morillat roughly parallel Caliban, Stephano, and Trinculo; Clarinda suggests Miranda. Both plays open with a storm at sea and a shipwreck. Both close with a recognition scene and a joyful departure from the island. But the magical atmosphere of Shakespeare's island has evaporated. The earthy poetry of Caliban has been debased into the gross hunger scene of II, 1, in its peculiar way one of Fletcher's grotesque masterpieces. The coarseness of this Fletcher-Massinger version has, on the whole, little to recommend it, but as a stepping-stone between the romantic comedy of Shakespeare and the Restoration theatre it does deserve some attention.

Though *Beggars Bush* (1615–22) has much this same coarse-grained quality, it far better suits this story of a merry gang of beggars. Again the collaborators drew on a Shakespearian situation in telling the story of Gerrard, deposed Earl of Flanders, who, to escape the usurper, flees to the woods and disguises himself as the king of the beggars. The adventures of Goswin, a noble merchant, furnish the material for the secondary plot, but it is the country interludes which make for the play's chief charm. (The rustic subplot of *The Fair Maid of the Inn* (1626) also partakes of this gaiety, though Biancha, the Fair Maid, has little of the genuine radiance of Bess Bridges, Heywood's Fair Maid of the West.) More often than not Fletcher's country folk, like Gerrard or Biancha, turn out to be exiled or mislaid aristocrats, but Higgen and Prig of *Beggars Bush* speak in the authentic accents of the English peasantry. They have something of the wit, humour, and poetry of Autolycus. Fond as he is of the courtly setting, Fletcher often satirizes it through rustic interpolations, and his excursions into the countryside sound an Arcadian note that recalls Webster's *Character of a Happy Milkmaid* or Walton's delightful landscapes. Fletcher's characters often masquerade in a Watteau-like *fête champêtre*, but the country-folk of *Beggars Bush* belong among the robust peasantry of a Breughel *kermesse*.

But of all the Fletcher-Massinger comedies of intrigue none surpasses *The Elder Brother* (1625) for sheer buoyancy and good humour. The play merits study also because of its relation to Congreve's *Love for Love*, the title of which seems suggested by the line: 'Can you love for love and make that the reward?' The story of the rivalry of two brothers, one a scholar and one a courtier, for the hand of Angelinna (Congreve's Angelica) and the efforts to disinherit Charles, the elder brother, make Congreve's debt obvious. The fact that this comedy is in prose further relates it to the later one. All in all, one wishes that Fletcher and Massinger had collaborated more often in comedies of this type, and the wooing scene in III, 5, which seems to have particularly impressed Congreve, indicates their capacity for writing love scenes without the coarseness which characterizes so much of their work.

Though H. D. Sykes has attributed to Massinger a share in *Henry VIII*, his arguments have been generally discountenanced. Both this play and *The Two Noble Kinsmen* now find general acceptance as the joint work of Shakespeare and Fletcher. That Shakespeare should have elected Fletcher as his co-partner in these plays has occasioned some understandable doubt. Yet these were the two leading playwrights for the King's Men. So close had been their association with the rise of tragi-comedy that their precedence as originators of this *genre* is still debated. Beaumont's retirement from the theatre in 1613 left Fletcher without the collaborator he constitutionally needed. Quite possibly Shakespeare, though he had previously shown no inclination to collaborate, at this time welcomed the opportunity.[8] He himself was contemplating retirement, and these plays indicate his weariness. They have been called 'an old man's plays'. Fletcher, whatever his deficiencies, had already demonstrated his merit as a collaborator. His share in *Henry VIII* is usually assigned as follows: I, 3–4, II, 1–2; III, 1–2; IV, 1–2; V, 2–5, though this assignment by no means satisfies everyone. Repeated feminine endings in these sections tend to substantiate this attribution, but, as Baldwin Maxwell has pointed out, other textual analyses seem to disprove Fletcher's participation or suggest that his work was modified by still another collaborator. Others find in *Henry VIII*, however, evidence of Fletcher's peculiar dramatic rhetoric, and, in an examination of the death scenes, Eugene Waith has noted Fletcher's tendency to fall into patterned verse with stereotyped sentiments. The tableaux are pre-arranged, the central figure needs only to step into them.

Nay, then, farewell!
I have touched the highest point of all my greatness;

And from that full meridian of my glory
I haste now to my setting: I shall fall
Like a bright exhalation in the evening,
And no man see me more.

(III, 2, 223–28)

Wolsey's farewell is echoed not only within the play, the lines also suggest the much-praised scene of Ordella's resignation to death in the nearly contemporary *Thierry and Theodoret.*

'Tis of all the sleeps the sweetest,
Children begin it to us, strong men seek it,
And kings, from height of all their painted glories,
Fall like spent exhalations to the centre.

(IV, 1)

Anyone who has read Fletcher realizes his penchant for writing fine lines—and writing them again. Similarly, the procession of magnificent shows in *Henry VIII* and its disjunctive and episodic nature are typically Fletcherian. From the banquet-scene to the trial, the coronation and the christening, the stage teems with the pomp and pageantry that proved so fatal to the Globe. Rarely does the play concentrate on the title figure. Indeed he often seems lost as the playwrights turn the spotlight first on Buckingham, then on Wolsey, and last of all on Cranmer, in the casual manner of the earlier chronicle play.

The Two Noble Kinsmen (1613–16) shares many of these characteristics. It is generally agreed that Fletcher's hand may be seen in the following scenes: II, 2–6, III, 3–6; IV, 1–2; V, 2. Again the emphasis is on spectacle, from the opening scene of Theseus and Hippolita's nuptials to the climactic invocation at the altar, but the play moves on two distinct levels. The grave and thoughtful pageantry of the Shakespearian opening ill accords with the glib manipulation of the Fletcherian portions of the drama. The Palamon and Arcite of Shakespeare are not the Palamon and Arcite of Fletcher.

In a brilliant article Theodore Spencer has pointed out the essential differences between Shakespeare and Fletcher which this play reveals.[9] Though Fletcher shows a sense of stage mastery and an accomplished style, his world is fundamentally a superficial one. The Palamon and Arcite of Shakespeare are thoughtfully, almost passively, conceived. Fletcher turns them into men of action rather than contemplation. Shakespeare's Palamon and Arcite have an existence independent of the scene. Fletcher's exist only for the particular moment. Fletcher gives us the experience; Shakespeare its interpretation.

The record of Fletcher's collaborations bears out the assumption that he took a casual view of playwriting and audiences. In his collaborations, after Beaumont's death, he made little apparent effort to exert himself. He drew upon the 'common stock of dramatic morality,' to use Lamb's phrase. He did not ask too much of the intelligence of his audience, though let us not forget it was an exceptional one. He and Massinger made use of the tried and approved dramatic formulas and conventions. Doubtless their audience was as skilled in assembling clues, penetrating tangled plots and predicting denouements as the television and cinema audiences of today. Disappearances and discoveries, disguises and revelations, these were for the spectator familiar devices. For this reason, perhaps, the playwrights increasingly sought out the sensational and *outré*.

Fletcher as a collaborator is easy to criticize, yet his collaborators must have found him a highly satisfactory one. He had the Midas touch. His self-imposed task was to amuse the restless and jaded coterie audience. His tricks and mannerisms served him so well that he saw little reason to exert himself in idle experimentation. If he was denied the supreme gift—and the metabolism—of genius, he had an extraordinary sufficiency of talent. It was enough for him, as it is enough for most playwrights, to entertain his audiences, and to Johnson's maxim, 'The drama's laws, the drama's patrons give,' he would have heartily assented.

NOTES TO CHAPTER FOUR

1. The Fletcher-Massinger collaboration is well discussed in Maurice Chelli's *Etude sur la Collaboration de Massinger avec Fletcher et Son Groupe*, Paris, 1926.

2. Roberta F. Brinkley, *Nathan Field, the Actor Playwright*, Yale University Press, 1928, pp. 93 ff.
3. Eugene M. Waith, *The Pattern of Tragicomedy in Beaumont and Fletcher*, Yale University Press, 1952, pp. 204–205.
4. Baldwin Maxwell, *Studies in Beaumont, Fletcher and Massinger*, University of North Carolina, 1939, p. 190 ff.
5. Lamb's note on *Thierry and Theodoret* in his *Specimens of the English Dramatic Poets.*
6. Maxwell, *Studies*, pp. 170–176.
7. Cleanth Brooks, 'A Note on the Death of Elizabethan Tragedy', *Modern Poetry and the Tradition*, University of North Carolina, 1939, pp. 203–218.
8. H. Dugdale Sykes, *Sidelights on Shakespeare*, Stratford-on-Avon, 1919, pp. 18–47.
9. Theodore Spencer, '*The Two Noble Kinsmen*', *Modern Philology*, XXXVI (1939), pp. 255–276.

FIVE

BEAUMONT AND FLETCHER IN THE RESTORATION

BEAUMONT and Fletcher serve as our chief link between the English theatre before and after the Restoration. After Fletcher's death in 1625 their plays continued to enjoy popularity and their works remained the chief dramatic staple of the King's Men. In 1641 they protested vigorously and successfully against a plan to publish twenty-seven Beaumont and Fletcher plays which they had in manuscript. During the same year, in the last days before the Protectorate and the closing of the theatres, Prince Charles commanded a performance of one of their plays. On January 6, 1641/42 the following entry appears in Sir Henry Herbert's dramatic records:

> On Twelfe Night, 1641, the prince had a play called The Scornful Lady at the Cockpitt, but the King and Queene were not there; and it was the only play acted at court in the whole Christmas.[1]

He had selected the play of Beaumont and Fletcher's that proved the most liked during the sunnier period after 1660. But even during the dark days of the Lord Protector's melancholy regime, and despite recurring anti-theatrical ordinances, the popularity of the two collaborators never suffered a total eclipse. Actors continued to perform, or tried to perform, their plays. In 1647 the sheriff of London raided a clandestine production of *A King and No King* in Salisbury Court; in 1648 The Red Bull distributed handbills advertising *Wit Without Money;* later in the same year a party of redcoats brought an abrupt end to a performance at the Cockpit of *Rollo, or The Bloody Brother.*[2] Kirkman's *The Wits* (1662) a collection of drolls acted by Robert Cox during the interregnum, also gives proof of their continuing popularity, for of the twenty-seven comic excerpts from Elizabethan and Stuart drama, fourteen derive from Beaumont and Fletcher. By 1647 the actors were compelled to part with their valuable manuscripts and under James Shirley's sponsorship the noble Folio appeared containing thirty-four Beaumont and Fletcher plays and one masque.

With the happy advent of Charles and the revival of the theatre, the playwrights once more came into their own. Though one would be hard put to find many points on which John Dryden Richard Flecknoe, and Jeremy Collier could agree, the recognition by all three of the part played by Beaumont and Fletcher in shaping the Restoration drama does represent such a point of convergence. 'Our plots are weaved in English looms; we endeavour therein to follow the variety and greatness of characters which are derived to us from Shakespeare and Fletcher,' wrote Dryden.[3] Richard Flecknoe, acknowledging the witty influence of Fletcher upon comedy associated him as well with another form of Restoration drama: 'Beaumont and Fletcher first writ in the Heroick way'.[4] Even Jeremy Collier tacitly assumed the continuity of tradition in the English drama and glumly contemplated its decline from its low estate under Shakespeare and Beaumont and Fletcher to its still greater degeneracy under Dryden and Congreve.[5]

Their recognition of this influence obviously did not prevent them from differing sharply as to its nature. Richard Flecknoe, though he praised Fletcher for his wit, felt the grave misgivings proper to a neo-classicist in the face of their breaches of decorum and confused characterization. A touch of Dol Common tainted their heroines; a 'witty obscenity' muddied their comedies. But for a full-scale attack we must turn to the works of Thomas Rymer.

The Tragedies of the Last Age Considered (1678) has become by now something of a joke in the history of dramatic criticism. Rymer, if he is remembered at all, survives as the critic who in his *Short View of Tragedy* (1693) reduced *Othello* to a warning to women to look well to their linen. A critic of the most limited vision, with a literal and humourless point of view, he nonetheless commanded real attention in his own day. As a neo-Aristotelian he found it painful to face the excesses and successes of *A King and No King, The Maid's Tragedy*, and *The Bloody Brother*. Corneille had, after all, been brought to heel by the French Academy's deliberation on the irregularities of *Le Cid*, and Racine's genius had flowered within the most circumscribed limits. It could only be lamented that Sidney had come too early to purge the Elizabethan drama and that Ben Jonson's precepts were, lamentably, revered rather than observed. In searching Beaumont and Fletcher for improbabilities and absurdities Rymer had not far to look. Violations of decorum and poetic justice met his eye on every page. Both his critical vocabulary and that of his disciple in aesthetics, Jeremy Collier, abound with the words 'unnatural' and 'improbable'. His castigation of Beaumont and Fletcher, absurd as it often is, nonetheless set the pattern for a whole school of neo-classical critics.

Whatever his excesses, Rymer could not be overlooked by his contemporaries. That his views commanded respect Dryden makes plain in his preface to *All for Love* and his *Heads of an Answer to Rymer*. His *Essay of Dramatick Poesie* (1668), published ten years before Rymer's attack on Beaumont and Fletcher, had expressed a generous estimate of their merit. Dryden's speculations on the stages of Athens, Rome, Paris and London led him to praise Fletcher for his wit and repartee and his excellence in representing the passions, 'above all, love'. The tragi-comedies, especially *A King and No King*, also excited his favourable comment. In the *Heads of an Answer to Rymer* Dryden amplified these liberal opinions by taking Rymer to task for too strict an adherence to the yardstick of the Stagirite. The theatrical amusements of Whitehall, after all, could scarcely be expected to correspond to those in the theatre of Dionysius. Though willing to concede the superior plotting of classical drama, Dryden remained obstinate in his admiration for the variety, resource, and good writing he found in the English drama.

But Dryden's apparent reluctance to publish his *Heads of an Answer* (it did not appear until the 1711 edition of Beaumont and Fletcher) and his deference to Rymer in transforming Shakespeare's Cleopatra from a gipsy trull to a Lely beauty indicate his critical respect for neo-classicism, if not his submission to it. Even before Rymer's attack on Beaumont and Fletcher, his enthusiasm for them had begun to cool, as the *Defence of the Epilogue* (1672) demonstrates. The preface to *Troilus and Cressida* (1679) also indicates his deepening awareness of the gap that separated Shakespeare from his contemporaries. Fletcher he reduces to no more than a limb of Shakespeare, and Fletcher's characters, contrasted to those of Shakespeare, he finds no more than 'pictures shown you in the twilight'.

Restoration audiences, however, were awed neither by the niceties of neo-classical criticism nor, as Pepys amply testifies, by the transcendent genius of Shakespeare. When Thomas Killigrew and William Davenant, the two patentees of the Restoration theatre, carved up between them the Elizabethan and Jacobean repertory, they drew almost entirely upon four playwrights—Shakespeare, Jonson, and Beaumont and Fletcher. For the next century their theatrical precedence was a matter of dispute. First one and then another took the lead in the long steeple-chase that came to an end only in the mid-eighteenth century. Only then was Shakespeare's pre-eminence finally established and only then did Bardolatry begin in earnest.

In 1660, certainly, Beaumont and Fletcher enjoyed many advantages. The Restoration temper did not incline, basically, toward tragedy. While *Hamlet* and *Othello* were great enough to survive any temporary mutations in taste, Restoration playgoers on the whole preferred the moral certainties of heroic drama to the complexities and ambiguities of Shakespearian tragedy. They preferred also the sensationalism of Beaumont and Fletcher's tragi-comedies to the chilly correctness of Jonsonian tragedy. In comedy Beaumont and Fletcher were equally attuned to the later audience. The romantic figures of Shakespearian comedy—Rosalind and Orlando—could not breathe freely in the airless drawing-rooms of Horner and Margery Pinchwife. Though the knavery and gulling of Jonsonian comedy suited the Hobbesian laughter of the Restoration audience, Beaumont and Fletcher's comedies appealed even more to their taste. The caste which the collaborators had favoured had reached its political zenith. The gay young blades and the pert heiresses who populated their comedies now dominated London society and had made the theatre their almost exclusive province.

Statistical analyses by Arthur Sprague and John Wilson bear out Dryden's remark that about two of Beaumont and Fletcher's plays were acted to every one of Shakespeare's.[6] Of the seventy-two plays performed by the King's Company during the period between 1660 and 1662, twenty-six derive from the Beaumont and Fletcher canon. Jonson's ran a poor third in production, if not in praise. The curve of the graph indicates that the two playwrights' popularity rose to a high level and remained high until approximately 1682. By that time the Restoration theatre had perfected its own comic tradition, and Otway and 'She-Tragedy' had begun to replace the heroic drama and tragi-comedy. During the period from 1682 to 1695 the popularity of the collaborators slowly began to diminish. Of their thirty-three plays produced prior to 1682 only fourteen were revived, six of them in altered versions. The defection of Thomas Betterton and his group of actors in 1695 accelerated the decline. Within the next two decades the patent Drury Lane company and the Lincoln's Inn Field company of Betterton produced only twenty-one of Beaumont and Fletcher's plays between them, half of them in altered form. As the stock of these two playwrights fell, that of Shakespeare rose correspondingly, and by 1710 Shakespeare had overtaken, though not yet outdistanced, his rivals.

By that time Ben Jonson was also giving them a close race. In 1660 he could scarcely challenge their precedence. The four great Jonsonian comedies popular during the Restoration—*Volpone, The Silent Woman, The Alchemist,* and *Bartholemew Fair*—were 'popular not because of their similarity to the later comedy, but in spite of their lack of such similarity'.[7] The strictures of Thomas Rymer and Jeremy Collier bettered Jonson's position, and increasing attempts to retailor Beaumont and Fletcher's work to conform to the unities attest to the growing admiration for Jonson. It took the form, however, of critical rather than popular acclaim. Even the most loyal of the sons of Ben, Thomas Shadwell, though he began his career under the flag of the humours and the standard of Jonson, Horace, and Aristotle was forced to make a retreat in the face of hostile audiences.

In the two main *genres* of Restoration drama between 1660 and 1680, comedy and heroic drama, Beaumont and Fletcher unquestionably had more influence than either Shakespeare or Jonson, though critics have disputed its extent. Their effect upon English comedy can be determined with some assurance. While the exact relationship of French and English comedy arouses continued discussion few dare challenge Dryden's assertion that the Restoration drama had fundamentally English origins. The genesis of heroic drama is a far more slippery topic. L. N. Chase in his study of its evolution scarcely mentions Beaumont and Fletcher, nor does Allardyce Nicoll in his history of Restoration drama. Corneille, Tasso, Orrerry, Davenant, and the French romancers take precedence as the founders of this *genre*.

Of these, Sir William Davenant has been generally recognized as the key figure in the development of heroic drama, and his *Siege of Rhodes* (1656) has taken on increasing historical, if lessening literary, importance. In his work many elements were fused. Davenant's interest in opera, his association with Inigo Jones and John Webb in the last great Stuart masques, his interest in epics, his exposure to Corneille and the *romans de longue haleine*—all of these *The Seige of Rhodes* reflects. It shows as well his youthful recollections of Beaumont and Fletcher's tragi-comedies.[8]

As regards plot and setting, tragi-comedy and heroic drama share a number of elements. Love and war dominate both types. Rival kings, usurper and pretender, and rival lovers, sacred and profane, serve as common sources of dramatic opposition. Against a background of war, with its distant and muffled drums, they play their parts. In both types of plays the action is intense and varied, marked by abrupt peripeteia and carefully manipulated, happy denouements. Both make use of non-English settings. Both deliberately remove to a world half-illusory, half-real—Fletcher's Sicily, Dryden's Peru—and both further this dramatic ambivalence by using material half-legendary and half-historical.

A comparison between the types of characters in both *genres* also suggests certain parallels. In both, the *dramatis personae* are recruited from the upper classes. True, Beaumont and Fletcher permit an occasional intrusion by a countryman, citizen, soldier, or servant for comic contrast or narrative purpose, but the heroic drama, even more exclusively the province of the *haut monde* of love and war, denies them even this rare admission. Both *genres* tend toward careful character balance—hero, heroine, villain, villainess—and calculated contrast between types. Two types of women dominate—the virgin and the termagant. They appear in *Philaster* (Arethusa and Megra), in *The Siege of Rhodes,* the germinal heroic drama (Ianthe and Roxolana), and in *The Indian Queen,* the archetype of that form (Orazia and Zempoalla).

It would be misleading, however, to try and overextend similarities of characterization. Dryden's avowed intent to arouse 'admiration' sharply differentiates his heroes from those of tragi-comedy. Dryden's Montezuma (*The Indian Queen*) has little in common with Beaumont and Fletcher's Philaster. True, both heroes vacillate, but the hero of tragi-comedy is essentially passive. Circumstances sway him first one way then another. The protagonist of heroic drama wavers between the two magnetic poles of love and honour, but once the more powerful of these has exercised its attraction, he becomes the man of action. His heroic prowess commands our 'admiration' as Philaster's helplessness cannot. Philaster relates not to Montezuma, perhaps the most typical of the heroic drama's protagonists, but to Aurengzebe, perhaps the least typical.

The dramatic tension, the cruel division between the dictates of love and honour, though often implicit in tragi-comedy, becomes explicit in the later drama. Amintor's dilemma—will he avenge Evanthe's ruin or acknowledge the kingly divinity of her ravisher?—foreshadows the clash of absolutes and the moral crises that dominate heroic drama.

The spectacular scenic features of heroic drama can be found as well in Beaumont and Fletcher. *The Island Princess, The Prophetess* and *Bonduca* particularly appealed to Restoration audiences. The first of these, effectively shortened in 1669, served both Nahum Tate and Pierre Motteux for operatic versions. *The Island Princess* and *The Indian Queen* share a vaguely exotic background that lends itself admirably to stage display. Betterton in revising *The Prophetess* took full advantage of the resources of the Restoration theatre by heightening Fletcher's already elaborate stage directions with a transformation scene and a climactic vision of 'four separate stages representing the palaces of two gods and two goddesses'. George Powell's *Bonduca* shares these characteristics, and the insertion of ballets and musical interludes into *The Rivals* (*The Two Noble Kinsmen*), *The Faithful General* (*The Loyal Subject*), *The Fool's Preferment* (*The Noble Gentleman*), *The Pilgrim* and *Valentinian* show how easily Fletcher's work could be adapted to treatment of this kind. One feels sure the author would not have demurred at these alterations. His fondness for spectacular finales and his penchant for flamboyant stage effects, particularly in his third acts, suggest that he himself would have taken full advantage of the technical resources of Restoration scenes and machines.

Beaumont and Fletcher's influence upon another important phase of Restoration drama, the comedy of manners, has been considerably discussed. Its extent and nature may well continue to excite speculation, but no one can deny the popularity of Beaumont and Fletcher during the 1660's and 1670's. Kathleen Lynch, recognizing this, finds, nonetheless, their influence a comparatively slight one on the development of the social mode of Restoration comedy.[9] In their comedies, she avers, Restoration writers found the raw materials, not the patterns, of later comedy. As she points out, Fletcher stands closer to the tradition of exuberant Elizabethan farce and romance than to the incipient comedy of manners. *Wit Without Money*, a comedy of London life, she cites as a happy change from Fletcher's usual melange of brash action and intrigue. (Not surprisingly, this proved one of Fletcher's most popular works between 1660–1710.) In this play and in *The Noble Gentleman* he sketches town and country society—but these Miss Lynch cites as exceptions.

One can hardly deny that Fletcher had not developed a concept of manners. During his lifetime the friction between old and new society, old and new money, and mores, had not yet fully developed. Even Middleton, with his sharply etched pictures of London life and society, concentrates on the surface and makes little attempt to dramatize the underlying clash of social attitudes. With Massinger we feel an increasing awareness of the division between the *nouveau riche* Mompessons and Villiers and the older, landed aristocracy such as the Pembrokes, his patrons. By Shirley's time the lines of demarcation are clearly drawn.

To acknowledge Fletcher's non-recognition of the concept of manners is not to deny his real influence, nonetheless, upon Restoration writers of comedy. Though only four of his comedies have their nominal setting in London, many more of them actually take place there. While he and Beaumont or Massinger may transplant us to Sicily, Paris, Madrid, or even Moscow, before long we are breathing the air of Jacobean London. This London has less surface realism than Jonson's or Middleton's. Like the Restoration dramatists, Fletcher sketches his background with a minimum of detail. The life-like characters he sets against it lend it truth and dimension.

Of these realistic types the most important common to both Fletcherian and Restoration comedy is the gay young blade. Yet the parallels between the Fletcherian sparks and the Restoration beaux must be carefully drawn. Fletcher's and Congreve's Mirabells (*The Wild Goose Chase* and *The Way of the World*) perhaps most effectively point up the contrast. Congreve's hero, carefully schooled in the tradition of manners, would scarcely recognize his high-spirited namesake, though they have certain features in common. In the first place, Fletcher's Mirabell stands quite apart from any special tradition. He remains an individualist, a non-conformist. Caprices dictate his behaviour, and Oriana tames him as a falconer teaches a wild hawk to stoop to the lure. Millamant has no such problem. Her problem is to discover the man behind the mask of manners.

The concept of wit also divides the two heroes. Though much praised for his keen dialogue, mercurial quickness and skill in making gentlemen talk like gentlemen, all qualities which recommended him to Restoration audiences, Fletcher could not serve as a model for 'wit'. Fletcher's young men rely on the pun rather than the epigram, their language has the vigour of life but not the veneer of art. They lack the self-consciousness of their Restoration descendants. Fletcher's Mirabell can neither thread the devious labyrinth of the sex-chase nor thrust and parry in the wit combats with the skill of his Restoration namesake.

Nevertheless, Fletcher's Mirabell has much in common with

the heroes of the first phase of Restoration comedy, while the comic dramatists were still drawing their portraits from life. However inartistic we may find Dryden's Loveby (*The Wild Gallant*) or Etherege's Sir Frederick Frollick (*Love in a Tub*), they show the rake as he was. Indeed Sir Frederick's adventures parallel Etherege's own closely enough to suggest that in this instance life was treading not far behind literature. In the second phase of Restoration comedy, brilliantly inaugurated by Etherege's Dorimant (*The Man of Mode*) we see the rake as he saw himself—a semi-idealized portrait. In the closing phase Congreve reminisces over dissipation recollected in tranquillity. His portrait of the rake is softened by time and memory. The realistic portrait of the earlier rake, with its coarseness and blemishes, hangs beside the retouched Lelyesque portrait of the man of fashion. Though Congreve's Valentine and Mirabell may disavow their ancestry and point out a lack of family resemblance, they are nonetheless sired by Dorimant and Sir Frederick who descend, in turn, from the heroes of Beaumont and Fletcher's comedies.

Some relationships between the high-mettled heroines of Beaumont and Fletcher and those of the Restoration can also be established. While Oriana in *The Wild Goose Chase* has perhaps most often been cited as an example of this type of heroine, an even better one can be found in the title character of *The Scornful Lady*, the most popular of Beaumont and Fletcher's comedies during the Restoration. This lady is the archetype of the emancipated young woman who appears again and again in their comedies—in *The Woman Hater* and *Monsieur Thomas*, for example—to indulge her witty resource at the expense of the male sex. Two collateral lines descend from her and reappear in Restoration comedy: the ladies of too-easy virtue, the Berinthias and Belindas, who stoop to folly and discover too late that they have given themselves too cheaply; and the heroines of more calculating virtue, the Harriets, Angelicas and Millamants, who observe the rules of the social game and in a series of artful manoeuvres finally checkmate their husbands-to-be. In both earlier and later playwrights the clash is fundamentally the same. Neither beau nor belle can submit to the yoke of wedlock. The surrender of will, the loss of liberty is as painful for the Scornful Lady as it is for

Millamant, the concept of romantic love as enticing as it is suspect.

One might make a case, as John Wilson does, for the Restoration inheritance of other female types; the cynical immoralist, the resourceful confidante, and the impudent maid. As Wilson admits, however, these make up the permanent personnel of comedy and would doubtless have found their way into Restoration drama had Beaumont and Fletcher never existed. One might draw up a list also of similar male types, but these would again be difficult to relate directly. Conspicuously absent in Beaumont and Fletcher are the pairs of antithetical characters so important to later comedy—the beau and the fop, the belle and the disappointed woman of fashion, the wit and the would-be wit. We can find no character balance in earlier *dramatis personae* to compare with that in Restoration comedy which depends so largely on the friction between true and false people and fashions. Fletcher's pretenders to wit do not construe wit in the same sense that Witwoud does. The absurdities of Sir Fopling Flutter (*The Man of Mode*) or the airs and graces of Melantha (*Marriage à la Mode*) would have no particular point in Fletcherian comedy. Within the social context of Etherege's and Dryden's comedies they do.

If the lowest common plot denominator of Restoration comedy, and most comedy, for that matter, consists of the love chase, Feltcher's comedies, as well, depend on amorous intrigue, often complicated by the misogyny of the hero or the misanthropy of the heroine. Fletcher's usual view of love, more typically expressed in *Cupid's Revenge* than in *The Faithful Shepherdess*, is a fleshly one that links him to the Restoration. His heroes and heroines have a genuine zest for the sex chase, as do their Hobbesian descendants, Ariana and Gatty, Courtall and Freeman in Etherege's *She Would if She Could.* Only in the last phase of Restoration comedy has this zest evaporated. Congreve's Valentine and Mirabell seem to have lost these predatory instincts. They play their part in the chase, but out of good manners more than anything else. They thread their way through the intricacies of the sex chase as they might follow a path through the intricacies of a maze.

The gulling devices, the marriages in which both parties mistake each other's identity, multiple disguises—these and others made up the common stock of seventeenth-century dramatic conventions which both Beaumont and Fletcher and the Restoration comic writers drew upon. The later dramatists, however, used them with a difference. They used these devices not only to heighten the plot and simplify the denouement. The dramatic materials of earlier comedy—cuckoldings, mismarriages, endowed estates—these served the dramatists of the comedy of manners as suitable social rewards and punishments.

In the silvery, ordered social world of Mirabell and Millamant Fletcher would have had little welcome. Earlier, he would have won Etherege's approval (the soubriquet 'Gentle George' did not always apply), and Wycherley might have recognized in Fletcher some kindred elements, but Congreve, the intimate friend of the Duchess of Marlborough, would have been embarrassed, one suspects, by his boisterous humour, his reckless spirits, his unpolished wit.

The decline of Charles II's popularity and the slow erosion of the Cavalier way of life corresponded to the dwindling reputation of Beaumont and Fletcher. As the Restoration developed a comic tradition of its own, it depended less and less on Fletcherian comedy. As Rymer's doctrines took increasing effect, enthusiasm for their tragi-comedies began to wane. Shakespeare was submitted to the ministrations of Dryden and Tate, and Restoration hands set about to reshape the work of the two collaborators. Davenant's version of *The Two Noble Kinsmen* (*The Rivals*) typifies the efforts to make Shakespeare and Fletcher conform. Though after 1688 the plays of Beaumont and Fletcher continued to enjoy some popularity, they had ceased to have any real influence on the English theatre.

NOTES TO CHAPTER FIVE

1. Joseph Quincy Adams, *Dramatic Records of Sir Henry Herbert*, Yale University Press, 1917, p. 58.
2. Leslie Hotson, *The Commonwealth and Restoration Stage*, Harvard University Press, 1928, pp. 26, 34, 40.

3. John Dryden, *Essay on Dramatick Poesie*, in *Dramatic Works*, London, 1931, I, p. 38.
4. Richard Flecknoe, *A Discourse of the English Stage* (c. 1663) in W. C. Hazlitt, *The English Drama and Stage*, London, 1869, p. 277.
5. Jeremy Collier, *A Short View of the Immorality and Profaneness of the English Stage*, 2nd edition, London, 1698, pp. 51–53.
6. Arthur C. Sprague, *Beaumont and Fletcher on the Restoration Stage*, Harvard University Press, 1926, part I; John Harold Wilson, *The Influence of Beaumont and Fletcher on Restoration Drama*, Ohio State University, 1928, Appendix.
7. Wilson, *The Influence of Beaumont and Fletcher*, p. 26.
8. James Tupper, 'The Relation of the Heroic Play to the Romances of Beaumont and Fletcher', *Publications of the Modern Language Association*, XX (1905).
9. Kathleen M. Lynch, *The Social Mode of Restoration Comedy*, New York, 1926, pp. 19–24.

SIX

BEAUMONT AND FLETCHER SINCE 1700

WILLIAM and Mary's accession to the throne brought about a theatrical revolution as well as a political one. The trumpet-blast of Jeremy Collier confirmed it. The aristocratic Stuart audience gave way to an increasingly respectable bourgeois audience. Critical admiration for neo-classicism and popular enthusiasm for Otway and 'She-Tragedy' contributed to the lessening reputation of tragi-comedy. The tragic plight of Philaster could not match the Roman dignity of Cato's, nor Aspatia's woe the pathos of Calista's. In like manner, the rise of Steele's exemplary comedy hastened the decline of Fletcherian comedy. Monsieur Thomas's escapades did not accord with the delicate sensibilities of Bevil Jr.

Although some Fletcherian comedies of pure intrigue continued to hold the stage, most eighteenth century critics either brushed Beaumont and Fletcher aside or overlooked them altogether. Steele praised *The Chances* and *The Humourous Lieutenant* in passing, John Dennis mentioned Fletcher only in a letter, and Johnson buried him in a footnote to his edition of Shakespeare. William Collins' *Epistle to Sir Thomas Hanmer* (1743) and the *Biographia Britannica* (1747) express the conventional view that Shakespeare mastered the manly passions while Fletcher's domain extended over the lesser, softer one. Though Garrick found one of his best parts in *The Chances* and *Rule a Wife and Have a Wife* continued to have occasional performances, interest in their work declined sharply.

During the latter half of the century critical opinion remained either mixed or indifferent. Thomas Seward, successor to Theobald in editing their works, pleaded for an independent judgment on the two collaborators whose proud misfortune it inevitably was to be judged alongside the giant figure of Shakespeare. George Colman in his 1778 edition of their works also showed a sympathetic approach and, found in them real theatrical virtues. But Hugh Blair disliked them, and Edmund Malone's studies in Shakespeare convinced him that Beaumont and Fletcher were mere pigmies by comparison and that the Restoration playgoers showed regrettable taste in preferring the collaborators' works. Monck Mason in his highly spasmodic *Comments on the Plays of Beaumont and Fletcher* (1797) urged, as Seward did, a more liberal consideration of these authors, but Charles Dibdin in his *Complete History of the Stage* (1800) rendered the majority verdict in finding 'more good sense in the construction of *Every Man in His Humour* than all the work of Beaumont and Fletcher put together'. Their plays, he felt, shared the disorder of the Spanish stage, and while Dibdin discerned some merit in *The Wild Goose Chase*, he found little else to commend in their work.

The neo-classical worship of Jonson had by then passed its peak, but Garrick's Stratford Jubilee and the editorial labours of Johnson and Malone had enthroned and, one might almost say, sanctified, Shakespeare. The other Elizabethans sank into deepening obscurity until Charles Lamb's happy ruminations in the British Museum's Reading Room revived interest in them. His *Specimens of the English Dramatic Poets* (1808) had undeniably stimulating effects in calling attention to the lesser dramatists of the golden age, but it also had unfortunate repercussions. In choosing 'scenes of passion', 'serious descriptions, that which is more nearly allied to poetry than to wit', and in seeking to illustrate 'what may be called the moral sense of our ancestors', Lamb measured the Elizabethan and Jacobean playwrights as poets and philosophers rather than as dramatists. As poets Beaumont and Fletcher often came up to his standards; as philosophers, hardly ever. But it is as dramatists that Lamb could not measure them. His emphasis on the 'poetic' at the expense of the 'dramatic' vitiated much of his criticism, subtle as it often is, and seriously misled a generation of would-be poetic dramatists. The critic who, indirectly or not, inspired countless abortive closet dramas, could not be expected to evaluate the work of Beaumont and Fletcher properly.

His friend Samuel Coleridge felt a similar distaste for the practical side of the theatre and a similar interest in Beaumont and

Fletcher. On one occasion he borrowed Lamb's 1679 Folio. He returned it later, enriched with copious marginalia. This volume, and Coleridge's own annotated copies of their works (the George Colman edition reprinted in 1811) provide us with a lengthy critical commentary. While Coleridge concedes that Beaumont and Fletcher are nearly always entertaining, in his notes to *Rollo, or The Bloody Brother* he sums up his two main objections to their plays: improbability of psychology and reasoning, and a lack of ideas. Like Lamb, he felt irresistibly compelled to measure them against Shakespeare, and in so doing he returned again and again to the fundamental problem of differentiating talent and genius. Of Fletcher's tragedies he writes:

> The writer was utterly incapable of Tragedy—and that such instances *ad contra* as may be brought, must be attributed to lucky Imitation of Shakespeare, tho' blind to the *essential* excellence (which easily may be notwithstanding the mind is struck with *accidental* beauties) of what he has imitated.[1]

The Prophetess epitomized for him anti-Shakespearianism. *The Loyal Subject* indicated the narrowness of Jacobean political opinion contrasted to Shakespeare's 'permanent politics of Human Nature'. *Rollo* weakly imitated *Richard III*. A comparison of *Richard II* and *Bonduca* brought him to the heart of the matter:

> The latter [Beaumont and Fletcher] you will find a well-arranged bed of Flowers, each having its separate root, and its position determined aforehand by the *Will* of the Gardener—a fresh plant a fresh volition. In the former an Indian Fig-tree, as described by Milton—all is growth, evolution, genesis—each line, each word almost begets the following—and the Will of the writer is an interfusion, a continuous agency, no series of separate Acts. Shakespeare is the height, breadth and depth of Genius: Beaumont and Fletcher the excellent mechanism, in juxtaposition and succession, of Talent.[2]

To use Coleridge's famous distinction between fancy and imagination, Beaumont and Fletcher achieve a genuine success on the lower level of fancy, but they lack the essence of poetic genius, the power of imaginative synthesis.

Coleridge found them wanting in minor respects also. A codification of the legend of good women in Shakespeare induced him to attempt a similar catalogue in Beaumont and Fletcher. Needless to say, he was disappointed. Almost without exception the heroines of the collaborators struck him as offensive and morally ambiguous. Virtue, as well as vice, had its price. Those heroines not actually strumpets in act he found 'strumpets in imagination'. He took offence also at the collaborators' servility to the Stuart doctrine of Divine Right and their lamentable tendency to pander to the base whims of the court of James I.

Victorian critics such as Henry Hallam and George Darley were scarcely more sympathetic. It was difficult to make Beaumont and Fletcher acceptable to Mrs Grundy, as Leigh Hunt found out when, following the example set by Charles and Mary Lamb in their *Tales from Shakespeare*, he culled their plays to salvage passages which could not offend either through their coarseness, improbability, or political blindness.

At the same time, other critics tentatively explored a different approach. Alexander Dyce's editorial comments to the 1843–46 edition of their plays, while often mere pastiches of romantic criticism, show occasional flashes of sympathetic insight and appreciation. Bodham Donne also takes a more flexible critical attitude and, while readily admitting Beaumont and Fletcher's many imperfections, suggests the need to measure their achievement in terms of the seventeenth century theatre. The plays, after all, had been written for the Jacobean stage, not for the Victorian study.

Critics such as these, pleading for relative rather than absolute critical standards, encouraged the historical approach which, in the latter part of the century, increasingly dominated criticism. William Poel's researches into the nature of the Elizabethan theatre correspond roughly with detailed historical studies of Beaumont and Fletcher. For the most part, these were bibliographical. The 1679 Folio has caused many a scholarly headache, and from the time of Fleay on, bibliographers have puzzled over problems of attribution and dating, and the establishment of a definitive canon and text. All in all, these nineteenth century scholars tended to treat the 1679 Folio like a vast ossuary. The problems of rearticulation were, indeed, formidable ones. But these bibliographers exhumed Beaumont and Fletcher rather than revived them, and their quarrels and disagreements tended to intimidate and discourage literary critics. In many ways, of course, these bibliographers and textual analysts made valuable contributions to scholarship, and the systematic analyses of metrics and the close textual studies paved the way for A. H. Bullen's unfortunately incomplete Variorum Edition of Beaumont and Fletcher (1904–12). More recent studies by Louis Wann, R. C. Bald and Baldwin Maxwell[3] have led to a greatly clarified notion of the Beaumont and Fletcher canon and given meaning to Aubrey's account of their collaboration:

> I have heard Dr. John Earles, since the Bishop of Sarum, who knew them, say, that Mr Beaumont's maine Business was to lop the overflowings of Mr Fletcher's luxuriant Fancy and flowing Witt.[4]

Textual studies have substantiated this contrast between the grave Beaumont, his verse an echo of the steady, marching line of the Elizabethans, and the nervous and energetic Fletcher, with his penchant for feminine endings, and his hectic, broken lines. Gradually Beaumont's, Fletcher's and Massinger's contributions to the 1679 Folio have been sifted, and gradually each has assumed an increasing individuality.

Other historical studies have also tended to bring them into sharper focus. Orie Hatcher's *John Fletcher* (1905) considers the dramatist as a practical man of the theatre, and her study anticipates those of Granville-Barker and others in demonstrating that the Elizabethans and Jacobeans did not write with one eye cocked toward posterity. Fletcher's hard-headed attitude toward the theatre was shared, after all, by Shakespeare, who would have had little patience with many of the romantics' views on poetic drama. It is doubtful that he would have shared Lamb's distress at confining Lear's madness to the boards of Drury Lane. Though in the opening chorus of *Henry V* he laments the inadequacies of the

Globe, he staged his play there nonetheless. Fletcher's equally down-to-earth sense of the stage and the audience Miss Hatcher discusses in detail. As she rightly infers, defects that may strike the reader glaringly upon the page, may be overlooked in performance.

This awareness of Shakespeare and Fletcher as practical men of the theatre also marks Ashley Thorndike's *The Influence of Beaumont and Fletcher on Shakespeare* (1901). Shakespeare's motivation for abandoning the tragic exaltation of Hamlet, Lear, and Othello in favour of the romantic distresses of Imogen, Hermoine, and Miranda has been interpreted variously. But Thorndike's study and Frank Ristine's *English Tragi-Comedy* (1910) attribute this primarily to Shakespeare's sense of theatrical fashion. Thorndike's conclusion that tragi-comedy owes its introduction and popularity to the collaborators has been generally accepted, though his second thesis, that the last Shakespeare plays are variations on themes previously expressed by Beaumont and Fletcher, is less generally believed.[5] Yet the recognition of this influence has done Beaumont and Fletcher much harm. The impression is often implicit, if not explicit, that but for their debilitating effect, Shakespeare's great tragic period might have been prolonged. The assumption is scarcely a justifiable one. We cannot predict what Shakespeare's course might have been without them, and except in contrast to such works as *Hamlet* and *Lear, The Tempest* shows little evidence of a decline.

A number of critics, however, have persistently viewed Beaumont and Fletcher as a contaminating influence not only on Shakespeare but on the period as a whole. Fletcher, in particular, they claim, once freed from the sobering influence of Beaumont, hastened the decline of the theatre from its robust Elizabethan health into lingering Jacobean infirmity. Charles Gayley's *Beaumont the Dramatist* (1914), a well-documented book, but over-literary in approach and markedly biased, vigorously attempts to absolve Beaumont of blame for the sins of his collaborator, whom Gayley finds chiefly responsible for the Jacobean decadence. His vindication of Beaumont had little effect, however, on Rupert Brooke. In his *John Webster and the Elizabethan Drama* (1916) he singles out Beaumont and Fletcher as glaring examples of those playwrights who deserted the solid Elizabethan terrain to drift off, rudderless, masters of a derelict vessel, across 'a sea of saccharine'. William Archer took as dim a view of their achievement, but for different reasons.[6] His reverence for Ibsen and the new drama led him to inspect and re-evaluate the English dramatic heritage and, not suprisingly, he found such dramatists as Beaumont and Fletcher inexplicably overrated. Examined in terms of 'material probability and psychological plausibility', as Coleridge discovered earlier, tragi-comedy crumbles into mere fustian. Aspatia and Mrs Alving, in more ways than one, do not speak the same language.

More recent critics have, on the whole, been kinder and Beaumont and Fletcher have attracted a fair share of sympathetic attention in the last thirty years. As Lamb kindled the romantics' interest in the Elizabethan playwrights, so T. S. Eliot has sparked a revival during our own day. However, his essay on 'Four Elizabethan Dramatists' specifically rejects both Lamb's predominantly poetic approach to drama and Archer's implicit assumption 'that a play need not be literature at all'. Eliot's call-to-arms for a restoration of balance between 'poetry' and 'drama' in poetic drama leads him to observe: 'The weakness of the Elizabethan drama is not its defect of realism, but its attempt at realism; not its conventions, but its lack of conventions'.[7]

On this point, Beaumont and Fletcher's success in creating a dramatic pattern and tradition, critics have divided sharply. Eliot, for one, feels that they did not succeed. Where Ben Jonson triumphed in developing his own conventions, in creating his own artificial but self-contained world, Beaumont and Fletcher failed.[8] Eliot's description of their verse bears this out: 'The blossoms of Beaumont and Fletcher's imagination draw no sustenance from the soil, but are cut and slightly withered flowers stuck into the sand'—a judgment reminiscent of Coleridge's. Both the universe and the poetry of the collaborators Eliot finds 'superficial, with a vacuum behind it; the superficies of Jonson is solid'. In short, Eliot condemns them for their lack of order and their reliance on momentary effect, and finds little method in their artifice, either in language or in dramatic conception. Instead of form, he finds mere amorphousness.

M. C. Bradbrook, in her *Elizabethan Tragedy* (1935), shares these convictions. She also finds the basis of the plays 'outrageous stimulation' dependent upon 'the maximum amount of sensationalism'. As dramatists not bound by a scheme either of moral values in tragedy or critical values in comedy, Beaumont and Fletcher move at will in the blurred and Protean world of tragi-comedy. Again and again Miss Bradbrook finds evidence that this moral anarchy has led to structural disorganization and the collapse of the poetic.

Yet it is precisely on the grounds of structure and convention that other critics have defended them. Una Ellis-Fermor's essay begins with the vigorous dissent: 'The work of Beaumont and Fletcher escapes from the tyranny of Jacobean incertitude into a world of its own creating'.[9] Avoiding the grandeurs of tragedy and the astringencies of satirical comedy, they succeeded, she finds, in creating a new type of play keyed in a 'middle mood'. Weakness of motivation and violation of character to heighten situation mark this world of tragi-comedy, yet these plays, she points out, have a formalized if precarious structure, and their world an order of its own.

The same realization underlies Lawrence B. Wallis' *Fletcher, Beaumont and Company* (1947). That these two practitioners of 'theatrecraft for the gentry' lacked Shakespeare's poetic genius and insight Mr. Wallis readily acknowledges. Yet, within their self-imposed limitations, he finds them playwrights of extraordinary talent in exploiting the Jacobean stage and Jacobean attitudes. He also recognizes their 'formality' and 'their discriminating, though baroque aesthetic quality'. Other critics, discussing the large outlines of seventeenth century movements in art, have also labelled tham 'baroque'.[10] One by one, the Elizabethan and Jacobean playwrights have been placed upon the baroque bed of Procrustes. It is hard to deny that it is less uncomfortable for Beaumont and Fletcher than for many others. Such transcendent figures as Shakespeare and Corneille lie uneasily upon it, but lesser figures lend themselves more easily to measurement of this kind.

That Beaumont and Fletcher's work has at least some affinities with this movement is evident. The nervous rhythms of their verse suggest the disjunctive nature of the baroque line, their multiple use of exterior physical disguise and inner psychological alteration mirror its perpetual flux and movement. Many of the commonplaces of baroque terminology apply equally well to Bernini or Beaumont and Fletcher—pomposity, ornamentation, the striving after effect. The surprises and reversals of tragi-comedy have much in common also with the evanescent baroque enchantments of Inigo Jones' court masques. In both the primary impulse is to dazzle and surprise. The creator takes into account not only the emotions of the characters on the stage but also the emotions of the spectators in the audience. Spectator and actor merge in characteristic baroque confusion. They do not, as in a more classically conceived theatre, have separate identities, with the audience invited to share, momentarily, in the individuality of the artist's independent creation.

How far one may press such analogies among the arts remains, of course, highly debatable. (It is difficult to relate Vanbrugh, the architect of Blenheim, to Vanbrugh, the author of *The Relapse*.) The tumult and lack of discipline in the baroque ill accord with the increasing awareness of the element of order in Beaumont and Fletcher. André Koszul, one of the chief students of the baroque impulse in their works, admits: 'Il y a beaucoup d'art dans ces amples écritures; un art bien formel, et convenu, mains du moins un art très soutenu'.[11]

Eugene Waith's *The Pattern of Tragi-Comedy in Beaumont and Fletcher* (1952) also recognizes the formal aspects of their art. Of all the interpretations of the collaborators, his is at once perhaps the most original and the most deliberately limited. Rather than examining them as poets, moralists, psychologists, or men of the theatre, Mr. Waith has concentrated upon them as rhetoricians. The results are often stimulating, and he has greatly clarified the previously fuzzy critical awareness of their contribution to tragi-comedy by relating their work to the traditions of Roman declamation. Mr. Waith finds their triumph pre-eminently one of technique. Within the framework of the highly devised and artificial situations suggested by the *Controversiae*, the dramatists found scope for their oratorical powers. His study, like that of Lawrence Wallis and Arthur Mizener, demonstrates how complete a mastery of form and convention they achieved.

But to recognize their skill as dramatic craftsmen and their success in pleasing their audience, is not necessarily to approve their methods, or the results of the methods. The school of detraction still thrives. John F. Danby in his *Poets on Fortune's Hill* (1952) takes as his starting-point Lamb's remark: 'After all, Beaumont and Fletcher were but an inferior sort of Shakespeares and Sidneys'. The thesis of his book, the disintegration and narrowing of a tradition, is a depressing one, largely because it has so much truth. This decline, the removal from the broad Arcadian lawns of Wilton to the stale anterooms of Whitehall, Danby measures in his closing chapters on *Philaster* and *The Maid's Tragedy*. Aspatia's plight symbolizes for him the *fin de siècle* sense of the age. This passing from the sunshine of the Elizabethan era into the twilights and shadows of the Jacobean period furnishes the major theme also for Alfred Harbage's *Shakespeare and the Rival Traditions*, a study of the popular versus the coterie theatres, and a reluctant introduction to the theatrical world of Beaumont and Fletcher.

Though not overlooked by critics in recent years, the two dramatists have suffered the greater humiliation of neglect by readers and producers. Their limited reading public may seem understandable enough. The clash between love, honour and Stuart doctrine has little immediacy for us. Yet Beaumont and Fletcher's world was also the world of Donne, with which we have found so many affinities. Granted that Beaumont and Fletcher lack the poetic capacity to illuminate the dilemma of man in a changing society as intensely as did the great Dean of St. Paul's, they still have much to offer us. Their fondness for sensation and shock, their emphasis on sex, their energy, brilliance and wit, even their coarseness, all recommend them to the modern temper. Their dexterity in form and language also recommends itself to a generation nurtured on the New Criticism.

But it is on the stage that they should ultimately be judged. Their plays were written not to be placed between boards but to be played upon them. When John Dryden, recollecting the blazing success of Chapman's *Bussy D'Ambois* in the theatre, took time to examine the play in his study, he found he had been 'cozened by a jelly'. In assessing Beaumont and Fletcher we are unfortunately not permitted the advantage of such a comparison. Though a surprising number of Beaumont and Fletcher's plays have genuine literary interest, still more might come to life upon the stage. It may be that our growing knowledge and use of the Elizabethan stage and Elizabethan staging will lead to a revival of interest in them. Let us hope so, for it is the spectator, above all, who can give us the truest evaluation of their achievement.

NOTES TO CHAPTER SIX

A detailed history of Beaumont and Fletcher's critical history since 1700 will be found in Lawrence B. Wallis' *Fletcher, Beaumont and Company*, New York, 1947.

1. Coleridge note on *Valentinian* in Lamb's copy of 1679 Folio of Beaumont and Fletcher now in the British Museum. See pp. 384-385.
2. Coleridge note in his own copy of *Works of Ben Jonson and Beaumont and Fletcher*, London, 1811, now in the British Museum. See vol. III, p. 413.
3. Louis Wann, 'The Collaboration of Beaumont, Fletcher and Massinger', *Shakespeare Studies by Members of the Department of English*, Madison, University of Wisconsin Press, 1916, pp. 147–174; R. C. Bald, *Bibliographical Studies in the Beaumont and Fletcher Folio of 1647*, Oxford University Press, 1938; Baldwin Maxwell, *Studies in Beaumont, Fletcher and Massinger*, Chapel Hill, University of North Carolina Press, 1939.
4. John Aubrey, *Brief Lives*, ed. Oliver Dick, London, 1950, p. 21.
5. For a recent opinion of this relationship see: '*Philaster* and *Cymbeline*', *English Institute Essays* (1951), New York, 1952.
6. William Archer, *The Old Drama and the New*, Boston, 1923, pp. 65–70.
7. T. S. Eliot, 'Four Elizabethan Dramatists', (1924) in *Selected Essays*, New York, 1932, p. 94.
8. Eliot, 'Ben Jonson' (1919), *Selected Essays*, p. 135.
9. Una Ellis-Fermor, *The Jacobean Drama*, London, 1936, p. 201.
10. André Koszul, 'Beaumont et Fletcher et le Baroque', *Cahiers du Sud*, X (1933), pp. 210–216; Mark Mincoff, 'Baroque Literature', *Annuaire de l'Universite de Sofia*, XLIII (1946–1947), pp. 1–71.
11. Koszul, 'Beaumont et Fletcher et le Baroque', p. 213.

CHECK LIST OF PLAYS

The First Folio (1647) of Beaumont and Fletcher includes thirty-three plays and, in addition, *Four Plays in One* and Beaumont's *Masque* which are not dealt with in this study. Of these plays, all previously unpublished, at least twenty-eight belonged to the King's Company. Six years before they had refused to permit publication of their Beaumont and Fletcher manuscripts, but times were unusually hard for actors in 1647. This group of plays, collected by James Shirley, does not, however, fairly represent Beaumont and Fletcher. The Second Folio (1679) is far more complete. It contains fifty plays, and also *Four Plays in One*, Beaumont's *Masque* and Shirley's *The Coronation*. I have included in the list three plays not found in the Second Folio—*Henry VIII, Sir John Van Olden Barnavelt,* and *A Very Woman*—since Fletcher is generally believed to have had some share in them.

This list, drawn largely from Alfred Harbage's invaluable *Annals of English Drama,* makes no pretence to be bibliographically exhaustive or original. I have arranged the plays in alphabetical order, followed by accepted or approximate date(s) of composition in parentheses, date of first publication, and presumed or known authorship. The letters B, F, and M designate Beaumont, Fletcher, and Massinger.

Barnavelt, Sir John Van Olden, (1619), 1883, F and M.
Beggars Bush, (1615–22), 1647F, F and M.
The Bloody Brother, (1616–24), 1639Q, F (M? Jonson? Chapman?).
Bonduca, (1609–14), 1647F, F.
The Captain, (1609–12), 1647F, F (B? M? Rowley?).
The Chances, (1613–25), 1647F, F.
The Coxcomb, (1608–10), 1647F, B and F.
Cupid's Revenge, (1608–12), 1615Q, B and F.
The Custom of the Country, (1619–22), 1647F, F and M.
The Double Marriage, (1619–22), 1647F, F and M.
The Elder Brother, (1625), 1637Q, F and M.
The Fair Maid of the Inn, (1626), 1647F, F and/or M (Ford? Webster?).
The Faithful Shepherdess, (1608–09), undated Q. c. 1609, F.
The False One, (1619–22), 1647F, F and M.
Four Plays in One, (1608–12), 1647F, B and F and Field.
Henry VIII, (1613), 1623F of Shakespeare, Shakespeare and F (and M?).
The Honest Man's Fortune, (1613), 1647F, F and M and Field (others?).
The Humorous Lieutenant, (1619), 1647F, F.
The Island Princess, (1619–22), 1647F, F.
A King and No King, (1611), 1619Q, B and F.
The Knight of the Burning Pestle, (1607–10), 1613Q, B (and F?).

The Knight of Malta, (1618–19), 1647F, F and M and Field.
The Laws of Candy, (1619–22), 1647F, M (revising B and F?).
The Little French Lawyer, (1619–22), 1647F, F and M.
The Lovers' Progress, (1623), 1647F, F and M.
Love's Cure, (1625), 1647F, M (revising B and F? Jonson?).
Love's Pilgrimage, (1614–22), 1647F, F (B? Shirley? Jonson?).
The Loyal Subject, (1618), 1647F, F.
The Mad Lover, (1615–19), 1647F, F.
The Maid in the Mill, (1623), 1647F, F and W. Rowley.
The Maid's Tragedy, (1608–11), 1619Q, B and F.
Monsieur Thomas, (1610–16), 1639Q, F.
The Nice Valour, (1615–25), 1647F, F? and Rowley? B? Middleton?
The Night Walker, (1609–14), 1640Q, F (revised by Shirley).
The Noble Gentleman, (1626), 1647F, F? (revised by Rowley?) and ?
Philaster, (1608–10), 1620Q, B and F.
The Pilgrim, (1621), 1647F, F.
The Prophetess, (1622), 1647F, F and M.
The Queen of Corinth, (1616–18), 1647F, F and M and Field.
Rule a Wife and Have a Wife, (1624), 1640Q, F.
The Scornful Lady, (1610–16), 1616Q, B and F (and M?).
The Sea Voyage, (1622), 1647F, F and M.
The Spanish Curate, (1622), 1647F, F and M.
Thierry and Theodoret, (1607–21), 1621Q, F and M (B? Field? others?).
The Two Noble Kinsmen, (1613), 1634Q, Shakespeare and F (B? M?).
Valentinian, (1610–14), 1647F, F.
A Very Woman, (1634), 1655Q, M (and F?).
A Wife for a Month, (1624), 1647F, F.
The Wild Goose Chase, (1619–22), 1652F, F.
Wit At Several Weapons, (1609–20), 1647F, F? B? Middleton? others?
Wit Without Money, (1614–20), 1639Q, F.
The Woman Hater, (1606), 1607Q, B.
The Woman's Prize, (1604–17), 1647F, F.
Women Pleased, (1619–22), 1647F, F.

A SELECTED BIBLIOGRAPHY

Bald, R. C., *Bibliographical Studies in the Beaumont and Fletcher Folio of 1647*, Oxford University Press, 1938.

Beaumont and Fletcher, *Works*, ed. Arnold Glover and A. R. Waller, 10 vols., Cambridge University Press, 1905–1912.

Bradbrook, M. C., *Themes and Conventions in Elizabethan Tragedy*, Cambridge University Press, 1935.

Chelli, Maurice, *Etude Sur La Collaboration de Massinger Avec Fletcher Et Son Groupe*, University of Paris, 1926.

Danby, John F., *Poets on Fortune's Hill*, London, Faber and Faber, 1952.

Ellis-Fermor, Una, *The Jacobean Drama*, London, Methuen, 1936.

Gayley, Charles, *Beaumont the Dramatist*, New York, Century, 1914.

Harbage, Alfred, *Shakespeare and the Rival Traditions*, New York, Macmillan, 1952.

Hatcher, Orie L., *John Fletcher*, University of Chicago Press, 1905.

Koszul, André, 'Beaumont et Fletcher et le Baroque', *Cahiers du Sud*, X (1933).

McKeithan, Daniel M., *The Debt to Shakespeare in Beaumont and Fletcher's Plays*, Austin, Texas, 1938.

Maxwell, Baldwin, *Studies in Beaumont, Fletcher and Massinger*, Chapel Hill, University of North Carolina Press, 1939.

Mizener, Arthur, 'The High Design of *A King and No King*', *Modern Philology* XXXVIII (1940–1941).

Oliphant, E. H. C., *The Plays of Beaumont and Fletcher*, Yale University Press, 1927.

Ristine, Frank H., *English Tragicomedy*, New York, Columbia University Press, 1910.

Spencer, Theodore, '*The Two Noble Kinsmen*', *Modern Philology*, XXXVI (1939).

Sprague, Arthur Colby, *Beaumont and Fletcher on the Restoration Stage*, Harvard University Press, 1926.

Tannenbaum, Samuel A., *Beaumont and Fletcher (A Concise Bibliography)*, New York, 1938.

Thorndike, Ashley H., *The Influence of Beaumont and Fletcher on Shakespeare*, Worcester, Mass., 1901.

Tupper, James, 'The Relation of the Heroic Play to the Romances of Beaumont and Fletcher', *Publications of the Modern Language Association*, XX (1905).

Waith, Eugene M., *The Pattern of Tragicomedy in Beaumont and Fletcher*, Yale University Press, 1952.

Wallis, Lawrence B., *Fletcher, Beaumont and Company*, New York, King's Crown Press, 1947.

Wilson, Harold S., '*Philaster* and *Cymbeline*', *English Institute Essays* (1951), New York, Columbia University Press, 1952.

Wilson, John Harold, *The Influence of Beaumont and Fletcher on Restoration Drama*, Ohio State University, 1928.

INDEX

GEORGE ALLEN & UNWIN LTD
London: 40 Museum Street, W.C.1

Auckland: 24 Wyndham Street
Sydney, N.S.W.: Bradbury House, 55 York Street
Cape Town: 58–60 Long Street
Bombay: 15 Graham Road, Ballard Estate, Bombay 1
Calcutta: 17 Chittaranjan Avenue, Calcutta 13
New Delhi: 13–14 Ajmeri Gate Extension, New Delhi 1
Karachi: Haroon Chambers, South Napier Road, Karachi 2
Toronto: 91 Wellington Street West
São Paulo: Avenida 9 de Julho 1138–Ap. 51